D1171851

POLICY STUDIES IN EMPLOYMENT AND WELFARE NUMBER 4

General Editors: Sar A. Levitan and Garth L. Mangum

Food for the Hungry: The Reluctant Society

Judith A. Segal

115894

The Johns Hopkins Press, Baltimore and London

Copyright © 1970 by The Johns Hopkins Press
All rights reserved
Manufactured in the United States of America

The Johns Hopkins Press, Baltimore, Maryland 21218
The Johns Hopkins Press Ltd., London

Library of Congress Catalog Card Number 79-133455

International Standard Book Number 0-8018-1227-5 (clothbound edition)
International Standard Book Number 0-8018-1226-7 (paperback edition)

Originally published, 1970
Paperback edition, 1970

This study was prepared under a grant from The Ford Foundation.

Contents

Preface

When Judith Segal became interested in food programs in 1966, the subject was not popular even in the Office of Economic Opportunity, where she worked. With her views set down in a terse book only four years later, food programs have already had their day and are fading in national interest. It must be that we are a senile society; problems that we cannot quickly capture or solve, our minds skip over. In the case of hunger, distraction is assisted by a variety of ready-made put-downs of poor people; Mrs. Segal begins her book with them. She knows what the first problem is and does not fail to convey a sense of outrage, however muted.

The book outlines the problem of the poor in securing food, and it makes plain how painfully slowly food programs are moving. Bowing to the analytic mood of the times and her own training, Mrs. Segal shows that children damaged by malnutrition will not be restored by Headstart. She shows that wiping out hunger is more efficient and productive than letting it persist. But clearly it is her view that hunger is wrong *because* it is wrong. She would spend inefficiently, even wastefully, if that were required to wipe out hunger. It is a coincidence, with which she hopes to persuade a greedy and self-absorbed people, that wiping out hunger is also efficient. She provides policy-makers what they ask, but her spirit is alive.

Mrs. Segal writes about freedom too—an uncommon idea to introduce into a discussion of feeding poor people. She thinks poor people ought to buy with cash in a free market, just like anybody! There is much here about improving the administration of food programs, and their auspices. As it happens, I do not agree with the implication of her concluding discussion—that for a long range solution we should look to a larger and drastically reformed public assistance program. I think myself that the long range solution is more complicated, involving social security, new cash programs that prevent poverty rather than fill a gap after people are poor, and a small public assistance program. But either way, the service of this book is to present technical analysis against a consciousness that other issues are determining—justice and freedom, in particular.

The British say of public officials that they must not only do justice; they must *be seen* to do justice. One would be moved to add a parallel statement: we must not only do right, we must do right for the right reasons. Hunger and malnutrition in a wealthy nation are a moral issue first of all. It will do nothing for our spirit to wipe out hunger in order to make ourselves richer. Conversely, we can wipe out hunger whenever our spirit requires it, even if we thought it not an efficient thing to do. There are no excuses.

Nor will anyone find excuses in this book.

Alvin L. Schorr

POLICY STUDIES IN EMPLOYMENT AND WELFARE NUMBER 4

General Editors: Sar A. Levitan and Garth L. Mangum

1

The Reluctant American

This is an unusual story. It is the story of an American *failure*. For many years this failure was obscured by the more familiar American success. American success should have made poverty and hunger an anachronism. America produced the necessary resources. It produced the necessary know-how. Apparently it did not produce the necessary motivation.

The discovery of hunger in America shocked a public which had taken for granted that free food was available to poor households. After all, food was one resource the country seemed to have more of than it needed; giving it away didn't cost much, probably not as much as it would cost to store it. The public did not know that when it came to the development and operation of the food programs, no one, in either the public or the private sector, had espoused the cause of the poor. The same could not be said for the farmers and the food distributors, both of whom had powerful lobbies to promote their interests in food consumption. The poor had no lobby. They were the target of food programs not simply because they were hungry, but because they were hungry enough to provide a vehicle for increasing the nation's food consumption, and to put additional income into the pockets of the farmers and food distributors.

While the Department of Agriculture paid lip service to feeding the poor, it never undertook a systematic investigation to find out whether its food programs were meeting the needs of the poor. Ignorance and apathy at policy-making levels characterized these distribution programs, and hunger persisted.

The failure of America to eliminate hunger and malnutrition among its citizens is part of the larger story of poverty in America. The failure of government efforts to feed the hungry is only partly attributable to the problems of bureaucracy. It is more significantly the result of a lack of commitment on our part to provide all Americans with an equal opportunity to achieve their share of American success.

Much of the recent controversy over hunger in America has emphasized the technical complexities of administering hunger and poverty programs and has ignored our reluctance to dip deeply into our own pockets to eliminate hunger and poverty permanently. Although we would like to believe that there is a common consensus to eliminate fundamental need in our society, we have provided ourselves with a number of myths to prevent any moral commitment from becoming too costly.

THE RUGGED INDIVIDUALIST

One of these myths is that most of us make our own way without help from the government. The man who went to public school, enjoyed the free school bus and the subsidized lunch program, went to a state college on the GI Bill, bought a house with an FHA loan, obtained a Small Business Administration loan for his faltering business, whose children were born in the county hospital built in part with Hill–Burton funds, whose parents are living on Social Security payments that amount to far more than they contributed to the program, whose money is in a federally insured bank, and whose son is attending school under the National Defense Education Act—this man will stand up in his local Chamber of Commerce, complain about public assistance expenditures, and say "I believe in rugged individualism. People should stand on their own two feet."

Contrary to common belief most government activities do not redistribute income to the poor. Tariffs, investment credits, farm commodity payments, expense account deductions, housing loans, etc., go to those who can afford to own property or be in business. Even income transfers, which are normally associated with re-distribution to the poor, go only in part to the poor.[1] Our whole system of income security is designed not to take people out of poverty but to keep middle- and upper-income people from falling into poverty. People who are unfortunate enough to be only sporadically employed throughout their lifetime are not entitled to unemployment compensation when they lose their job or to Social Security benefits when they reach old age because they were unable to pay the "premiums." Public assistance payments are a small portion of the amounts paid out in income transfers. In fact, the distribution of income in this country has not changed significantly in the past 20 years.

THE POOR IN SPIRIT

Another one of the myths we perpetuate to keep our antipoverty budget down is the "poor in spirit" theory. It goes like this. Even if the poor had money, they would not have the taste or knowledge or whatever is required to improve their life style. We maintain that people are poor from "the 'unwise use of resources,' originating in 'ignorance, from a wrong set of values, from shiftlessness or from a broken spirit.' Whatever the cause, successful treatment of such families must include the 're-education of habit and emphasis upon right standards—through personal influence.' "[2]

Further, since we believe that the poor will not obtain what they *need* in the face of the ever-present temptations to buy what they

[1] Robert J. Lampman, *How Much Does the American System of Trans-fers Benefit the Poor?* (Institute for Research on Poverty, University of Wisconsin, 1967).

[2] Roy Lubove, *The Struggle for Social Security, 1900–1935* (Cambridge, Mass.: Harvard University Press, 1968), p. 108.

want, we insist that it is appropriate for us to provide them with what we think they need rather than with an income that would permit them to make their own "mistakes," as the rest of us do.

Food and other in-kind programs are a direct result of this belief. The *Washington Post,* one of the nation's most respected liberal newspapers, has during the recent hunger colloquium published two "solutions" to the hunger problem which indicate that this myth is far from dead, even among the intelligentsia.[3] Both articles advocated distribution of food instead of money as a solution to the hunger problem. Miss Logue, in some economic sophistry based on the theory of inferior goods, suggested that all grocery stores distribute free food items that would be packaged in olive drab with black stencilling that says "U.S. Government Free Food" to discourage the nonpoor from "accepting" the gift—a program which she claims has no means test! To convince the poor that lard, bulgur, beans, and skim milk would be a boon to their lives she relates that the Marquesa de Merry del Val, wife of the Spanish ambassador, prefers beans to caviar, and that bulgur wheat is sold in the gourmet departments of local supermarkets as "wheat pilaf." Both articles agreed that food stamps will not solve the problem because "they are lacking in educational content." Miss Logue was particularly disturbed by a young woman in front of her in the checkout line who bought cokes and candy with food stamps.

Considering the monotony of their diet and the little money they have for more extravagant recreation, the poor have better reasons to drink cokes and eat candy than the rest of us who every week purchase enormous amounts of overpriced, foodless "snacks," even though we have the education to know better and the means with which to buy nutritious alternatives.

Why do we insist that poor households be more informed and more disciplined about nutrition than we are? Chances are that we achieve a nutritious diet simply because we spend enough on

[3] Agnes E. Meyer, "How to Halt the Slow Murder of Children," The *Washington Post*, April 27, 1969, C3; Ruth Logue, "A Free Basic Diet for Every American," The *Washington Post*, July 27, 1969, B1.

food to provide a margin for error. That we begrudge a poor family its soda pop is indicative of our generally punitive attitude toward people we believe deserve their miserable circumstances.

The preoccupation with income-in-kind programs completely misses the point that no agency outside the home can efficiently make the numerous decisions required to provide a family with its needs. The inefficiency of trying to make these decisions for low-income households has proved far more costly in terms of both money and the perpetuation of dependency and poverty than the "mistakes" which households occasionally make in undertaking this endeavor for themselves. Such mistakes are inevitable in all households, but we only deny the freedom to make them to the poor. As a matter of fact, the Department of Agriculture's 1965 Food Consumption Survey indicates that poor households get more nutrition for their food dollar than other households do, and studies of food stamp participants show that they spend their bonus on nutritious foods, not luxuries.

On the basis of the "poor in spirit" myth, we have justified many years of trying to eliminate poverty without spending significant amounts of money. As recently as 1962, Congress passed legislation designed to improve the living standards of persons who were attempting to live on grossly inadequate public assistance payments by giving them more social services.

THE SLUGGARD

Another one of our myths is that most of the poor are in that condition because they will not work. On the contrary, however, most working-age male heads of poor families are employed, as Table 1 indicates. More than half of these men work full time, but they remain poor because they work predominantly at low-skill jobs which do not pay an adequate wage. A full-time worker earning the minimum wage has an annual income of less than $3500. Millions of family heads in this country earn less than the minimum wage. Many of these men are working part-time because they cannot get full-time work.

Table 1.   Work Experience of Male Heads of Poor Families, 1966

	Total	Under age 55	Aged 55–64	65 or over
Didn't work	1,465	212	256	997
Ill, disabled	574	120	172	282
Other	891	92	84	715
Worked part year	1,132	777	180	175
Unemployed	470	372	69	29
Other	662	405	111	146
Worked all year	1,606	1,275	199	132
Total	4,203	2,264	635	1,304

SOURCE: Mollie Orshansky, "The Shape of Poverty in 1966," *Social Security Bulletin*, March 1968, Table 7.

In case we happen to believe that these families are being cared for by welfare payments, we should note that less than 1 percent of public assistance recipients are employable males. In any case, the acknowledgment, even by a conservative administration, of the total inadequacy of the present public assistance program to meet the minimal needs of the poor has deprived us of our chance to pretend that we are meeting our responsibilities through this program.

THE SCAPEGOAT

There has been much talk about hunger and malnutrition in America over the past three years. For the most part, however, the discussion has been limited to what is wrong with the government—why it has been so ineffective in assuring all Americans an adequate diet. But the issue of hunger in America cannot be separated from the issue of poverty in America.

Government policy has accurately reflected our limited commitment to eliminate hunger, just as it has reflected our lack of commitment to eliminate poverty. Our attempt to put the onus of the failure of the family food programs on the Department of Agriculture is no more convincing than the attempt to blame the social worker for the failure of public assistance. Some of the undesirable effects of program operation may be the result of unimaginative administration in both of these cases, but the basic elements of program design are a reflection of our own punitive attitudes toward the poor and our reluctance to accept collective responsibility for these societal ills.

The issues involved in the development and administration of the federal family food programs must be put into context. The government must work within a framework of objectives given to it by society. Its administration of programs can be effective or ineffective, depending upon the imagination and technical skills of the bureaucrat. But no matter how skilled administration may be, it cannot achieve objectives which the whole society is not prepared to support.

In a Senate hearing, after a group of doctors described starving children in Mississippi, Senator Javits asked Secretary of Agriculture Freeman: "What is really wrong here that the United States of America cannot get off the dime and cannot get itself wound up to do what must be done?" Senator Javits directed his question in the wrong direction; he should have asked his constituents.

2

The Hunger Crisis

It was hard for most Americans, whose "chicken in every pot" long ago became "two cars in every garage," to believe that there were people in this country who still did not have their chicken.

During the final years of the 1960's, at least three congressional committees investigated the problem of hunger and malnutrition in the United States. In 1968 the federal government began for the first time in its history a nation-wide nutritional status survey. In his first month in office President Nixon initiated an emergency food stamp program to enable destitute families in a few areas to obtain free food stamps. Yet, Robert Sherrill, whose article in the *New York Times* in 1967 initated the Great Hunger Discovery, had to conclude in his March 1970 sequel that "we are about as far as ever from achieving the national goal of three squares a day for everyone."[1] In fact, the stage is only now being set for the operation of an adequate food stamp program.

The hunger issue came to the attention of Washington in the winter of 1966, when Congressman Resnick of New York made a tour of Mississippi and wrote congressional and administration

[1] Robert Sherrill, "It Isn't True that Nobody Starves in America," *New York Times Magazine,* June 4, 1967; "Why Can't We Just Give Them Food?" *New York Times Magazine,* March 22, 1970.

leaders about the desperate straits of the poverty-stricken Negroes there. When the mechanization of cotton horticulture, the government's cotton support program, and an increased minimum wage brought twentieth-century "progress" to their nineteenth-century life style, these Negro families were left completely without income. There was no reasonable expectation that help would be forthcoming from their own communities. Their former employers looked upon them as "dead wood" for which no future use could be anticipated—or as one planter put it, "field hands are as useless as a mule."

Shortly after Representative Resnick's trip, a number of Negro families invaded the abandoned Greenville, Mississippi, Air Force Base. "We are here because we are hungry and cold and we have no jobs or land," was their explanation. The federal response: the Department of Defense moved in troops to evict them, and the Department of Agriculture moved in two experts to study the hunger situation in the Delta. The troops, to no one's surprise, had little trouble evicting the desperate Negroes from the air base, and the experts had no trouble finding many more families in the same position—cold, hungry, with no place to go. The Department of Agriculture, however, did not move to improve its food programs in these areas or to institute an emergency food program.

In July 1967, the Senate Subcommittee on Employment, Manpower, and Poverty was ready to hold hearings on the hunger issue. The stage had been set a month before by Robert Sherrill in his article, "It Isn't True that Nobody Starves in America," which included a full-page picture of yet another Washington expert, Robert Kennedy, discussing conditions with some of the local folk—who must have been thinking by this time of all the food they could have bought with the money used to transport these hunger discovery missions to the Delta and home again. Riding on the publicity of the Kennedy trip, the subcommittee blasted off with testimony from four doctors whose vivid descriptions of starving children in the south sounded like a report from an African country just out of the tribal stage.

10

In child after child we saw: evidence of vitamin and mineral deficiencies; serious, untreated skin infections and ulcerations; eye and ear diseases, also unattended bone diseases secondary to poor food intake; the prevalence of bacterial and parasitic disease, as well as severe anemia, with resulting loss of energy and ability to live a normally active life; . . . We saw homes with children who are lucky to eat one meal a day—and that one inadequate so far as vitamins, minerals, or protein is concerned. We saw children who don't get to drink milk, don't get to eat fruit, green vegetables, or meat. They live on starches—grits, bread, Kool-Aid. Their parents may be declared ineligible for commodities, ineligible for the food stamp program, even though they have literally nothing. We saw children fed communally— that is by neighbors who give scraps of food to children whose own parents have nothing to give them. Not only are these children receiving no food from the government, they are also getting no medical attention whatsoever. They are out of sight and ignored. They are living under such primitive conditions that we found it hard to believe we were examining American children of the twentieth century.[2]

Month after month went by with no action from federal officials, whose major alibi appeared to be that nobody knew exactly how many hungry people there were. Arguments about target populations and potential enforcement problems overshadowed the fact that there were indeed hungry people.

The Secretary of Agriculture, in testimony before Congress, claimed that numerous economic, legal, and administrative constraints (some actual, some imagined) had tied the department's hands in its attempt to feed the poor. One look at the niggardly supplements in the food programs convinced the administration that help from Congress was necessary if the programs were to be significantly improved, but neither President Johnson nor the Department of Agriculture were anxious to risk alienating the farm bloc, which had shown a distinct distaste for financing "welfare programs" with money that belonged to farmers.

The Citizens' Crusade Against Poverty, a labor-and foundation-

---

[2] U.S., Congress, Senate, *Hunger and Malnutrition in America, Hearings* before the Subcommittee on Employment, Manpower, and Poverty of the Committee on Labor and Public Welfare, United States Senate, 90th Cong., 1st sess., July 1967, p. 46.

financed community action group, under the pseudonym Citizens' Board of Inquiry into Hunger and Malnutrition in the United States, published their "documentation" of hunger in the spring of 1968.[3] It presented in both words and illustrations a picture of hunger, malnutrition, and poverty in many areas of this country, recommended sensible changes in the food programs, and indicated on the basis of a poverty index 256 counties which were most likely to have pockets of hunger. But this was not a documentation in the statistical sense and was considered by many federal officials to be a public relations snow job.

Congressman Poage, Chairman of the House Agricultural Committee, was so insulted by the CCAP accusations that he asked the health officer in each of the 256 "hunger counties" listed in their report if there were any hungry people in his jurisdiction. The replies which he received contained the usual hedging, the usual myths.[4]

For example, much was made of the distinction between "starvation" and "hunger," as if there were a public responsibility to feed people only if one could be certain that hunger would last long enough to kill them. The doctors who had reported to the Poverty Subcommittee had not hedged this point:

We do not want to quibble over words, but "malnutrition" is not quite what we found; the boys and girls we saw were hungry—weak, in pain, sick; their lives are being shortened; they are, in fact, visibly and predictably losing their health, their energy, their spirits. They are suffering from hunger and disease and directly or indirectly they are dying from them—which is exactly what "starvation" means.

Ignoring the serious implications of problems described in many of the letters, Poage summarized the responses: "In not one single county of those responding were there current cases of starvation reported." He conceded that "there were stories of people,

[3] Citizens' Board of Inquiry into Hunger and Malnutrition in the United States (Citizens' Crusade Against Poverty), *Hunger, U.S.A.* (Washington, D.C.: New Community Press, 1968).

[4] U.S., Congress, House, *Hunger Study,* Committee on Agriculture, U.S. House of Representatives, 90th Cong., 2d sess., June 1968.

especially children, suffering malnutrition" but "few instances of hunger as a result of inability to buy food or receive public assistance." Hunger always seemed to be attributable to the ignorance or the undesirable behavior of the poor, seldom to the fact that people simply did not have enough money to buy food. He continued:

The few reported cases of starvation which had occurred in the past were believed to have resulted from *deliberate negligence* by parents. Almost all of the hunger and malnutrition cases were blamed on *ignorance* by parents as to what constituted a balanced diet. . . . *Jobs were available in a community, but rejected by able-bodied men* who apparently preferred to remain on welfare rolls. . . . Families on food relief often had *television sets* and *nice automobiles*. . . . The head of the household was reported to be spending money on *whisky* that was needed for the purpose of food for the children. . . . An *unwed mother* with a number of children leaves two or three infants in the care of an older daughter, perhaps only 9 or 10 years old. . . . (Italics added.)

Representative Poage had "proved" there was no hunger problem. After all, there were limits to what one could do for the undeserving poor. Criticism of the Department of Agriculture's food program policy had therefore been "harsh and unwarranted."

The Poor March on Washington in the spring of 1968 made hunger its central issue. The Department of Agriculture made an awkward and limited response. It was reported that a major address by President Johnson himself offering a more generous package never materialized because the president did not want to appear to be responding to the pressure of Resurrection City, which by then was engulfed in mud and militants and was threatening to turn into Insurrection City. The opposition of the march leaders to the war also did not endear them to the president. Apparently, much of the passive response to the food crisis by the Department of Agriculture, as well as the Office of Economic Opportunity, was dictated by the White House.[5]

[5] Elizabeth B. Drew, "Going Hungry in America," *Atlantic*, December 1968.

In May 1968, the Columbia Broadcasting System presented a television documentary, "Hunger in America,"[6] which gave many Americans their first look at hunger. Theory became reality. Hungry faces were harder to forget than words. The CBS program stimulated a sizable flow of letters, one of which was written by Secretary of Agriculture Freeman to the president of CBS. Freeman complained that the program had "undermined the hope of the poor and hungry by implying that no one cares, least of all their Government," and he asked for network time "not . . . to defend the Department and its programs" but to correct this "disservice to the poor people, to the family farmers of America [whose commodity programs had been "attacked and ridiculed" by the program], and to the viewing public."[7]

CBS did not give Freeman equal time, but in a rebroadcast of the program the next month, it gave the Department of Agriculture credit for taking some significant steps since the first broadcast to improve the food programs. It had a few kind words for itself, too. Charles Kuralt reported at the end of the rebroadcast:

Representative Albert H. Quie of Minnesota asked Rodney E Leonard, chief of the Department's Marketing and Consumer Services if the CBS news broadcast had stimulated [Agriculture's] action. Mr. Leonard answered, 'It always helps to be pushed.'

In fact, a few days before the rebroadcast, Freeman had asked the House Agricultural Committee for an unlimited expansion of the food stamp program, infuriating Congressman Poage who obviously, contrary to usual procedures, had not been consulted on the action. Nevertheless, Secretary Freeman did not seem to be as appreciative of the CBS publicity as his aide. He characterized the program as "a disgraceful travesty of facts. . . . If you looked at that program, you'd think that nothing was being done, nothing

[6] The script of the CBS documentary "Hunger in America" was reprinted in the *Congressional Record* (Daily Edition), July 9, 1968, E6281-86.
[7] Letter from Orville Freeman, Secretary of Agriculture, to Dr. Frank Stanton, President, Columbia Broadcasting System, June 12, 1968.

had been done, and that there were ten million people in the United States that are hungry and starving. That just isn't true."

THE SEARCH FOR NUMBERS

Was it so absurd to think that as many as 10 million people were not getting enough to eat? On the basis of the Department of Agriculture's own food consumption survey, it has been estimated that more than 9 million low-income *households* in the United States have inadequate diets (Table 2). The department's survey, though inappropriate for determining actual nutritional status, which requires health as well as diet information, has been the only source of nation-wide data on which to estimate the prevalence of poor diet in the population. The percentage of deficient diets in the various income groups, as shown by the 1965 survey, is indicated in Table 3. Note that not only the rate but the seriousness of deficiencies are greater at the lower income levels, as indicated by the average number of nutrients in each group that are below the recommended allowances. In fact, the survey showed that 36 percent of the households with incomes under $3,000 a year had diets that provided less than two-thirds of the NRC allow-

Table 2. **Number of Households with Deficient Diets, 1965–66**

Annual Income	Number of Households	Households with Diets Less than Allowance for One or More Nutrients		Households with Diets Less than ⅔ Allowance for One or More Nutrients		Total Deficient Diets
		Per-cent	Thousands	Per-cent	Thousands	Thousands
$ 0–999	3,850,000	26	1,001	44	1,694	2,695
$1,000–1,999	5,822,000	23	1,339	39	2,271	3,610
$2,000–2,999	4,800,000	31	1,488	29	1,392	2,880
			3,828		5,357	9,185

SOURCE: U.S. Bureau of the Census, *Current Population Survey 1967* (1966 income); U.S. Department of Agriculture, *Household Food Consumption Survey 1965–1966.*

15

Table 3. Diet Inadequacy by Household Income, 1965

Annual Income Level	Percentage of Diets Below Allowance for One or More Nutrients	Average Number of Nutrients Below Allowances
$10,000 & over	37	1.9
$ 7,000–9,999	44	2.0
$ 5,000–6,999	47	2.2
$ 3,000–4,999	57	2.2
$ 2,000–2,999	59	2.5
$ 1,000–1,999	62	2.5
$ 0–1,000	70	2.5

SOURCE: U.S. Department of Agriculture, *Dietary Levels of Households in the United States, Spring 1965; Household Food Consumption Survey 1965–1966.*

ance for one or more nutrients, compared to 20 percent for households at all income levels. Almost one-half of the households whose incomes were less than $1,000 a year had a similarly poor diet.[8]

Dr. Jean Mayer, one of the country's leading experts on nutrition, later chosen by President Nixon as his White House consultant on nutrition problems, testified before the McGovern committee (the Senate Select Committee on Nutrition and Human Needs) in December 1968 that

the undeniable fact is that all the nutrition literature that we have, that is piling up every day, shows that we are dealing with many millions of people and I think it becomes really a matter of detail as to whether this is 10, 15, or 20. To think that one is only dealing with a few individuals who are too lazy or too ignorant to go to the county seat and get food stamps is really completely and totally unreasonable. It is unreasonable, first of all in terms of what we do know about the income of a great many Americans.[9]

[8] The under-$3,000 income category does not correspond to the official poverty lines, which vary for family size. Using the $3,000 classification underestimates the number of poor in large families and overestimates the number of poor, aged individuals with deficient diets. Both of these groups have higher than average rates of dietary inadequacy.

[9] U.S., Congress, Senate, *Nutrition and Human Needs, Hearings* before the Select Committee on Nutrition and Human Needs of the United States Senate, 90th Cong., 2d sess., Part 1, December 1968, p. 24.

On the basis of income alone, the McGovern committee concluded that more than 14 million Americans were suffering from hunger and malnutrition and that the more than 10 million remaining poor "probably suffer from periods of nutritional deficiency and they are continually at risk."[10] The committee compared the incomes of poor households with the cost of buying the Economy Diet developed by the Department of Agriculture, the standard upon which the official poverty lines are based. The Economy Food Plan is a translation of the National Research Council's diet adequacy standards into the quantities and types of food compatible with the food patterns of families in the lowest third of the income range. It calls for a minimum daily expenditure of about 84 cents per person in a family of four with two schoolchildren and consists mostly of dry beans, flour, and cereal.

The McGovern committee explained that about one-fifth of the 25 million poor Americans live in households that actually have a total income below the cost of the Economy Diet. Another 9.3 million live in families whose incomes are less than twice the equivalent of the Economy Diet. (The poverty lines are calculated at three times the cost of the Economy Diet.)

On what basis did Secretary Freeman reject these estimates?

The Department of Agriculture objects to using income to determine how many are hungry or malnourished because it believes that many of the poor have an adequate diet. It rejects the food survey as indicative of the number of hungry or malnourished people because it says that many poor families have inadequate diets because they are *unwilling*, not because they are *unable*, to buy a balanced diet.

THE DATA GAP

Why haven't we been able to produce some irrefutable statistical evidence of the prevalence of hunger and malnutrition in our so-

[10] U.S., Congress, Senate, *The Food Gap: Poverty and Malnutrition in the United States*, Interim Report together with Supplemental, Additional, and Individual Views, Select Committee on Nutrition and Human Needs, United States Senate, 91st Cong., 1st sess., August 1969, p. 20.

17

ciety? Surprisingly enough, the nutritional status of the population has never been an object of study. No one and no government agency has ever examined on a nation-wide basis how our diet has affected our health. The reason goes back to a number of historical precedents and institutional developments that have since the beginnings of our nation diverted our attention from the subject of hunger.

Widespread malnutrition has never been an obvious problem in this country. Traditionally, any hungry people that did exist have been a responsibility of local welfare authorities whose interests were restricted to their own community. When the federal government did enter the picture in the Depression, its food distribution programs were administered by the Department of Agriculture, which was interested primarily in increasing national food consumption and only incidentally in poor relief. Food program administrators did not demand nutritional status data because they did not conceive of their program as a systematic attack on hunger.

A nation-wide nutrition study would have required the collaboration of health and diet research teams, but the responsibilities for public health and the responsibility for food programs were separated in the bureaucracy. No one had a vested interest in a nation-wide nutrition study. The Public Health Service, after years of studying malnutrition abroad, recently initiated the first nation-wide nutritional status survey. This study is currently being undertaken in a limited number of states and is eventually slated to encompass enough states to yield nation-wide data, with emphasis on the poor.

Technical problems have also been responsible for the gap in our nutritional status data. No theory has been developed to predict the effects of changes in nutrient intake on the overall performance of an individual. The effects of single nutrient deficiencies, diseases like rickets and scurvy, have been assessed, and their impairment of particular body organs and their influence on growth, development, and resistance to disease have been established. But the study of individual nutrient deficiencies is unrealistic, in that many health problems are caused by multiple nutrient deficiencies or by interrelated nutrient and health deficiencies. The lack of a scientifically established relationship between food intake and the individual's total performance makes a definitive nutrition adequacy standard an unattainable goal at the present time. In other words, we are unable to say with any accuracy just how much a person needs to eat to maintain good health.

Although definitive standards of dietary adequacy have not been established, some educated guesses based on what we know about minimum needs in most individuals have been published by the US Interdepartmental Committee on Nutrition for National Development and by the Food and Nutrition Board of the National Research Council (NRC). The NRC values, defined by age and sex for normally active persons and designed to afford a margin of sufficiency above average physiological nutrient (but not caloric) requirements, are the most commonly used. They are not, however, uniformly related to minimum needs.

The lack of agreement among experts is demonstrated by the variations in nutritional standards among different countries. For example, the NRC standard for Vitamin C for an adult is 70 milligrams per day; the British Medical Association recommends 20 milligrams per day.

One of the problems of defining standards is deciding whether "adequacy" should be based on a minimum, optimum, or intermediate level of need. Minimum nutrient requirements can be defined as those which prevent clinical symptoms of dietary deficiencies, but many experts object to using minimum requirements because they feel a safety factor should be added to allow for individual variations. Minimum needs vary substantially from one person to another, depending on such environmental factors as climate and such individual factors as size, age, activity, and capacity to utilize particular foods. Experiments have shown that individual protein requirements can vary from 21 to 65 grams a day, the difference amounting to more than 7 eggs or 6 ounces of sirloin steak.

In spite of the fact that nutritional standards are not definitive, the back of any cereal box will indicate that we commonly use

19

them, usually in terms of recommended daily allowances which include a margin of safety over the minimum standards. In fact, the official poverty lines are based on the NRC standards used in the Economy Food Plan, and the Department of Agriculture food consumption survey uses them to estimate diet adequacy.

The use of the NRC standards in the department's survey is qualified by the Food and Nutrition Board in this way: "It should not be assumed that food practices are necessarily poor or that malnutrition exists because the recommendations are not completely met." The Department of Agriculture adds its qualification: "Two-thirds of the allowance for any nutrient is considered a level below which diets *could* be nutritionally inadequate for *some* individuals over an *extended* period of time." (Italics added.)[11] The lack of definitive standards makes the department's survey results difficult to interpret.

Aside from the lack of definitive dietary adequacy standards, there are many other technical problems involved in obtaining an accurate picture of the country's food consumption. Distinguishing individual from family intake, measuring the nutrition content of various foods, and keeping track of alternative sources of nutrients such as vitamin pills are just a few.

The reliability of the food intake data is reduced by imperfections in the techniques used to obtain them. Neither the "recall" method, in which the subject is questioned about the family's food consumption in a past period, nor the "record" method, in which the subject keeps a current diary of what the family consumes, provides absolutely accurate data. In addition to the fallibility of the respondent's memory, there are difficulties in estimating the quantity and quality of food purchased or eaten away from home, in determining the nutrients wasted in storage, cooking and serving, and in estimating individual consumption from family data.

A fundamental problem involved in using the department's food

[11] U.S. Department of Agriculture, *Dietary Levels of Households in the United States, Spring, 1965,* A Preliminary Report (Washington, D.C.: Government Printing Office, 1968), pp. 4–5.

consumption survey to estimate the prevalence of malnutrition is that it does not provide any data on the health of the population. Determining an individual's nutritional status requires information about both his health and food intake. Information about food intake alone is not sufficient to predict whether his health is suffering because his diet is inadequate in terms of published minimum requirements.

Because of the lack of definitive diet adequacy standards, the problems of obtaining accurate data on food intake, and the lack of health data, many experts feel that nutritional shortages reported in this type of study are not as serious as they appear to be. They claim that investigations of food consumption, particularly on a regional and national scale, do not consider many of the factors which lessen the chances that an individual will suffer damage to his health from a diet that is *on the average* inadequate. They offer as support for their position, first, that established dietary allowances allow a margin of safety, and, second, that environmental factors may alter the amount of a particular nutrient required.

The Impasse

Congress and the administration used the uncertainty about the extent of hunger and malnutrition to postpone a major attack on these problems. It is doubtful, however, whether an accurate estimate of the number of hungry and malnourished persons is even relevant.

It is not logical, in terms of the national policy objective of eliminating poverty, to distinguish between the poor who have inadequate and the poor who have adequate diets. It is impossible to separate the problem of hunger and malnutrition from the problem of poverty. The impasse between the administration and the critics of the government's food programs is caused to a large degree by the fact that the critics are talking primarily about poverty and the government is considering the food programs in a much narrower framework. That is why the critics call for food

21

programs which are essentially income supplement programs, and both the Johnson and the Nixon Administrations have considered such programs extravagant.

The White House Conference on Food, Nutrition, and Health (notice that the word "Hunger" is not included) brought this disagreement into the open. The White House set up special panels on various aspects of the hunger and nutrition problem to make recommendations to which the bulk of conference participants could react. These panels consisted of people with established interests in the food, nutrition, and health areas. Established interests do not necessarily prevent a person's thinking objectively about the issue at hand, and, in fact, the ideas of these people were valuable because of their detailed knowledge of how the system is presently working. However, working close to a problem is likely to limit one's ability to consider drastic innovative solutions to it, and the recommendations of the panels showed this type of myopia. Most of the panels discussed and recommended unimaginative solutions related to the normal professional functions of panel participants—nutrition education for the home economist, food enrichment for the food processors, and food purity law enforcement for the bureaucrat. These prosaic recommendations stimulated a critique by "voluntary action task forces," which published their evaluation of the recommendations shortly before the conference was convened.[12] One of the task forces wrote:

All the other problems of nutrition fade into insignificance beside the fact that 25,000,000 Americans, or more, are living on an income that prevents them from getting enough to eat. . . . The true cause of hunger and malnutrition is poverty—not ignorance, lack of education, willfulness, inadequate food supplies, but poverty.

This critique went on to disparage many of the resolutions that

[12] *Panel Recommendations of the White House Conference on Food, Nutrition, and Health,* November 1969 (draft); *Preliminary Views of the Voluntary Action Task Forces to the Provisional Draft of Panel Recommendations to the White House Conference on Food, Nutrition, and Health,* November 1969.

he original panels had proposed. For example, the numerous proposals by the original panels for nutrition education elicited his statement from one of the task forces:

Because poverty, and *not* lack of education is the main cause of hunger and malnutrition, we discourage extensive expenditures on formal nutrition education. In any case, the most efficient and inexpensive way to provide nutrition education is to provide food.

It should be noted that not all of the responding task forces advocated innovative outlooks. The task force of farm organizations gave an explicit statement of the traditional philosophy:

The citizens of the United States are blessed with having ample supplies of wholesome, high quality food as compared to anywhere in the world. Agriculture is dedicated to the continued production of this food at reasonable prices to the consumer. However, the consumer should realize that future food supplies are going to be contingent upon the economic return to agriculture.

These task forces for the most part, however, gave priority to providing an adequate income for the poor. Some gave specific recommendations for improving income maintenance programs. Only as a short-run substitute for such action did they suggest improvements in the food programs. These ideas permeated the actual conference and resulted in a more spontaneous and illuminating confrontation of issues than usually emerges from White House conferences, which tend to enhance reputations more than knowledge. Out of the White House conference, therefore, came the proposal for a $5500 minimum income guarantee. This figure left far behind the $1600 minimum income level proposed by President Nixon in his Family Assistance Plan, even with the proposed food stamp supplement which could amount to as much as $700 or $800.

GRAVY FOR BREAKFAST

The National Welfare Rights Organization, a group of AFDC mothers who have been a major influence in the effort to reform public assistance programs, was in large part responsible for the conference's explicit recognition of the fact that the real issue at hand was poverty. These mothers have first-hand knowledge of the difficulties of living on an inadequate income. Their testimony brought home to a middle-class professional audience the reality of the hunger problem, not in terms of vitamins and minerals, but in terms of children who eat gravy for breakfast.

It is not difficult to determine that most families presently living on public assistance have little chance to achieve an adequate diet. Public assistance food budgets are generally based on one of the two low-cost food plans developed by the Department of Agriculture. The Economy Plan, actually an emergency plan suitable only for a limited period of time, has been described previously. The second plan, known as the Low-cost Food Plan, allows about $1 a person to be spent daily for food in a family of four with two schoolchildren. Both of these food plans require a knowledge of food purchasing, preparation, and nutrition that could be reasonably expected of a home economist. They allow for only a minimum of discard and plate waste and assume that meals will be planned by the week and that food will be bought in weekly quantities. These plans also allow the same expenditure for food eaten out as for food eaten at home, so that lunches at work and school that, of course, could not be bought as cheaply as meals made at home, reduce the home food budget. The Department of Agriculture itself has estimated that only about 25 percent of the families spending as much as the Low-cost Diet calls for are likely to obtain a nutritionally adequate diet.

To make matters worse, many welfare departments, while officially "budgeting" on the basis of these food plans, actually pay recipients less than these food plans call for. A special study of welfare food allowances in Cook County, Illinois, a state with a liberal public assistance standard, indicated that the food allowance for persons on welfare, even with food stamps, was not enough to purchase the minimally adequate diet devised by the County Department of Public Aid. The food allowance for adults is 26 cents per meal. Illinois uses the Economy Diet, the one suitable "for temporary or emergency use" to calculate its food allowance. Public assistance allowances often do not take into consideration sales taxes and price increases.

In a poor household, an adequate diet can be purchased only at the sacrifice of some other necessity, and it is most often the food budget that suffers, simply because it is more flexible than rent or utilities. Contrary to the Department of Agriculture's belief that many poor households are simply unwilling to spend enough on food, *all* poor households with an inadequate diet have a good reason for it. Further, since poor households with an adequate diet have achieved it at the sacrifice of some other necessity, it is particularly ironic that they should be denied government help just because it happens to be in the form of a food program. Of course, poor families that already have an adequate diet do not need help in the form of a food supplement. Offering them one gives them the incentive to spend their money elsewhere and collect their adequate diet from the government.

This points up the futility of trying to separate the effort to eliminate malnutrition from the effort to eliminate poverty. It is difficult to eliminate malnutrition when other types of inadequacies remain because the family will usually raid the flexible food budget to pay for other necessities. In fact, eliminating poverty is a more efficient way to eliminate malnutrition than providing food because it attacks the cause, not the symptoms, of malnutrition.

Although we have no reliable statistical estimates of inadequate diet among the poor, events of the past three years have brought to light empirical evidence that makes it impossible for us to deny that malnutrition is a serious problem for many families and that marginal diets are threatening the health of a sizable portion of our population. These families are unlikely to be able to obtain a better diet without some improvement in their economic situation. The relevant framework for the consideration of food programs is, therefore, not the size of the malnourished population but the contribution which such programs can make to the elimination of poverty. That we do not know how many people are hungry or malnourished becomes a moot point. We do know how many people are poor.

THE COSTS OF MALNUTRITION

There is now an increasing body of evidence suggesting that malnutrition in young children can cause permanent brain damage. Young children suffering from severe undernutrition during their early years when the brain is developing (about the first three years of life) might never realize their inherent intellectual potential because of permanent damage to the brain. The National Institute of Neurological Disease and Blindness in its collaborative perinatal project involving over 55,000 mothers has reported that maternal malnutrition may be the single most important cause of a host of subtle birth defects from lower intelligence to speech and hearing impediments.

Recent findings of two unusual studies which have followed a number of children over a considerable period of time have added strong support to the suspected relationship between malnutrition in young children and retarded intellectual development.

A three-year study of children in a small Mexican village has shown that 37 children hospitalized as babies with severe malnutrition scored lower on I.Q. tests at age 5 than their siblings who had not had serious nutritional deficiencies.[13] A similar study in South Africa showed that 20 children who had been severely malnourished as infants scored lower on I.Q. tests than a control group.[14]

Trying to establish the exact influence that malnutrition has on intellectual functioning is difficult because of the problems associated with controlling social and psychological variables that may also have some influence on intelligence. The Mexican study is particularly useful in this respect because it used a sibling com-

[13] "The Toll of Hunger on a Child's Intelligence," *New York Times*, March 17, 1970.
[14] M. B. Stock and P. M. Smythe, "The Effect of Undernutrition During Infancy on Subsequent Brain Growth and Intellectual Development," *South African Medical Journal* (October 28, 1967), 1027–30.

26

parison group, which establishes a good control over many important environmental variables. Dr. Herbert Birch, one of the chief researchers in the Mexican study, spoke of the hunger and poverty to which the children in his study were subjected: "These 'insults of environment' are lasting. They affect the child throughout life."

The words of Dr. Robert Cole, a noted psychiatrist and authority on malnutrition and poverty, are eloquent testimony to the fact that these "insults of environment" leave an indelible mark on the victim and on society.

I am describing in detail what it means for a child (and his or her parents) to be sick more or less all the time and hungry more or less regularly. That children can "adjust" to such a state of affairs goes without saying. They become tired, petulant, suspicious and finally apathetic. One can talk with them and play with them and observe their behavior and ask them to draw or paint pictures and from all that learn how the aches and sores of the body become for the child of four or five more than a concrete physical fact of life, but—in the child's mind—a reflection of his worth, a judgment upon him and his family by the outside world. They ask themselves and others *why*—what they have done to keep them from the food they want, or what they have done to deserve the pain they continue to feel. When the rest of us miss a meal or two, or experience a stomach ache or an injury we are moved to do something about it—and succeed in evading the irritability and annoyance and anger we may quite naturally feel. Consider what it means for a child to grow up without doctors for his complaints, without the dependable and balanced diet we take for granted.

In my experience with families in the Delta—some of whom I've known and observed for many years—their kind of life can produce a chronic state of mind, a form of withdrawn, sullen behavior that the word "depression" only begins to describe. I have seen some of the families I know in the South go North and carry with them that state of mind; they get more food, more welfare money, and in the public hospitals of Northern cities certain minimal medical services—but as one tape-records their expressed feelings and attitudes month after month, as I am now doing in a Northern ghetto, one sees how persistently sickness and hunger in children live on in adults—who doubt any offer, mistrust any goodness or favorable turn of events as temporary and ultimately unreliable. I fear that we have among us hundreds of thousands of people who have literally grown up to be

27

and learned to be tired, fearful, anxious, suspicious, and (as a physical fact of life) in a very basic, inflexible and tragic sense, *unbelieving*.[1]

Through its effect on an individual's ability to absorb an education or to attend school, malnutrition may vitiate all of society' attempts to equalize economic opportunity through education.

Making schooling available is ineffective unless a child is well enough to attend. Malnutrition can affect the motivation and responsiveness which any child needs to establish good learning habits. Brain-damaged children do not have the capacity to absorb an education; listless, apathetic children cannot establish the basic learning habits they need to carry them through school; nutritional deficiencies in older students affect their motivation to perform any task requiring self-discipline. "Apathy can provoke more apathy and contribute to a cumulative pattern of reduced adult-child interaction with adverse consequences for learning and behavior' is the way the experts explain it.[16]

An unpublished 1965 survey of 2,000 Chicago first-graders found that children who went without breakfast had trouble socializing in school, one of the basic first grade tasks. A principal in one of the schools studied said that "whenever we have a behavior problem, we find it helpful to review the last 24 hours of a child's life, especially what he ate." One of the teachers who had recently volunteered for work in this ghetto school said that it took her only a week to realize that "hungry kids don't learn."[1]

Economists measure the costs of malnutrition in terms of death and disability in the population. The reduction in economic and social productivity resulting from death and disability can be measured as the loss to society of future income or the value of

[15] U.S., Congress, Senate, *Hunger and Malnutrition in America, Hearing* before the Subcommittee on Employment, Manpower, and Poverty of the Committee on Labor and Public Welfare, United States Senate, 90th Cong. 1st sess., July 1967, p. 52.

[16] Nevin S. Scrimshaw, "Nutrition and Mental Development" (paper presented at the 25th Anniversary Commemoration of the Nutrition Foundation, Inc., Symposium, Cambridge, Mass., 1966).

[17] Linda Rockey, "Teachers See Daily Evidence that Hungry Pupil Don't Learn," in *Hunger in Chicago*, Chicago Sun-Times, April 1969.

28

future services. The costs of additional welfare and service programs which may be incurred when malnutrition causes physical and mental disability are also included. This is not, however, a very satisfactory measurement of the costs of malnutrition.

First, it is impossible to estimate for the United States how much of the cost of ill health and death is due directly or indirectly to malnutrition because the prevalence of malnutrition is unknown, and the role of malnutrition in the contraction and course of infection is not clear. It is likely that estimates derived from morbidity and mortality data are low, since most of the malnutrition in the United States is sub-clinical, and the influence of malnutrition on the course of disease or infection is often not readily apparent even to trained specialists. Few states collect data on malnutrition in their official health statistics, and mortality records do not indicate the true death rate from nutrition deficiency diseases.

Second, some social and economic costs which could be attributed to malnutrition are not counted when foregone productivity is measured solely in terms of premature death and disability. One of these subtle costs is the sub-optimum productivity of individuals who are unable fully to utilize their potential skills due to physical and mental fatigue brought on by undernutrition. A number of situations brought on by famine or wartime seiges have produced evidence that economic output is reduced when calories are reduced. If the calories are inadequate for the activity undertaken, the body will adapt to lower caloric intake by avoiding effort. Malnutrition leads to lack of ambition, an inability to concentrate, poor judgment, loss of self-discipline, irritability, etc., and social relationships as well as economic productivity are often changed for the worse by the resulting changes in motivation and personality.

Another subtle cost of malnutrition is the reduced intellectual capacity of individuals whose learning ability and motivation were affected by undernutrition in their early years. The sub-optimum performance of these individuals does not show up in mortality or morbidity statistics.

Probably the most important reason that the economists' measurements of the costs of malnutrition are inadequate is that productivity losses are not the most significant criteria upon which to base priorities for government action to eliminate hunger. A society which places a high value on the rights and well-being of individuals may determine that the social losses suffered from sickness and death are more important than the economic ones. It is not sufficient in such a society to measure the loss of a mother's "services" or the costs of a deformed body in the monetary terms of reduced income.

3

Diet Decisions in the Poor Household

Deficient diets are significantly more prevalent and more severe among low-income households. Poverty creates both market and motivational obstructions to the achievement of an adequate diet.

THE POOR PAY MORE

Low income forces many poor consumers to shop where prices are higher. Higher prices and the poorer quality frequently found in low-income shopping areas means poor households often get less nutrition for their money.

Studies have shown that as much as 35 percent of low-income households, compared to 14 percent of other households, shop for food outside of chain or discount stores.[1] Lower physical mobility and the need for credit generally offered only by higher-priced, service-oriented stores are probably the major reasons why many low-income people do not shop in the lower-priced stores.

Economies of scale in food consumption are more prevalent at

---

[1] Marcus Alexis, Leonard Simon, and Kenneth Smith, *Some Determinants of Food Buying Behavior* (Rochester, N.Y.: College of Business Administration, University of Rochester, 1967), p. 6.

higher income levels.[2] Patrons in low-income areas tend to purchase certain items in smaller sizes at higher unit cost, perhaps because they lack the money to buy the economy sizes. Storage facilities, especially refrigerator and freezer space, is limited. Rats and roaches make it impractical to store groceries on open shelves.

Food stores in low-income neighborhoods have been accused of discriminatory pricing policies such as raising prices on days when welfare checks are received. Although a government survey found no significant differences in prices charged by food stores in low- and higher-income areas when the same type of store was compared, the House Committee on Government Operations placed some doubt on the price data gathered in this survey because it was learned that stores were notified in advance of the price survey. The survey did indicate that prices were usually higher in the small independent stores, which are most common in low-income neighborhoods, than they were in large independents and chain stores, which predominate in the higher-income areas.[3]

Data obtained by private citizens' groups has shown price differences between chain stores in poor and upper-income neighborhoods. A consumer survey conducted by a community action group in Detroit found that inner-city chains had prices 3 to 5 percent higher than their counterparts in the suburbs and concluded that because many of the poor had to shop in corner groceries, since chains and large independents were not available, they paid from 20 to 40 percent more for their groceries.[4]

The Government Operations Committee in its own survey found that supermarket chain-store outlets sold food items of lower quality in the inner-city areas of Washington, New York City, and St. Louis than in outlets located in middle- and upper-

[2] James Freund, "Consumption Patterns Among the Poor," paper written for The President's Commission on Income Maintenance Programs, 1968, pp. 60–62.

[3] U.S. Department of Labor, *A Study of Prices Charged in Food Stores Located in Low and Higher Income Areas of Six Large Cities, February 1966*, Bureau of Labor Statistics (Washington: Government Printing Office, 1966).

[4] *Focus: Hope '68* (Detroit: Focus: Hope, Inc., 1968).

income areas. It concluded that while evidence before the committee that shoppers pay higher prices at food chainstores in poverty areas was not conclusive, it was sufficient to cause the committee great concern and to warrant immediate attention by the responsible federal agencies.

The committee also found practices in the retail sale of food by inner-city supermarket chain stores which they indicated may "contribute to the poor paying more" such as: the absence of meaningful competition; the bonus incentive system whereby the income of certain chain-store employees is dependent, in part, on the profit of an outlet; the absence of effective audit and inspection procedures directed to the maintenance of price and quality uniformity throughout all outlets; human error in making, changing, and checking price markings; placement of the most effective and experienced employees in middle- and upper-income area stores.

The Poor Family Responds

Since low income is responsible for much of the diet inadequacy in poor households, lowering the price they have to pay for food appears to be a reasonable method of improving their diet. The federal government initiated its food relief efforts in the Depression. Its programs have, in effect, lowered the price of a diet supplement to zero. But the poor household's response to programs which offer it an opportunity to increase its food consumption has not been encouraging. Numerous factors operate to dampen the response of low-income households to opportunities to improve their diet, even when they realize it is deficient, so that rarely is more than a third of any income increase spent on food.

Competition for the dollar

Probably the most important constraint the low-income household faces is its unsatisfied basic nonfood needs. In poor households the opportunity cost of food expenditures is high. The extent to which the household can maintain its freedom to choose be-

33

tween food and nonfood consumption is important in inducing it to take advantage of the opportunity to improve its diet. If it receives a price reduction, for example, only if it will divert some of its nonfood expenditures to food, the household may refuse to take advantage of it, even if the price has been reduced to zero.

Participation in the food stamp program is very low among eligible households because the program does restrict their choice between food and nonfood consumption. In this program the Department of Agriculture establishes, by budget and food consumption studies, the amount a family of a certain size, composition, and income should spend for food. For this amount, known as the purchase requirement, eligible families can buy food stamps at a discount. These stamps can be exchanged in any certified retail grocery store for any food product except packaged foods identified as imported.[5]

The purchase requirement is based on average food expenditures and may be more or less than any particular family in this income range actually spends for food. The family must spend its full purchase requirement each month to receive the bonus stamps. This provision assures that the household will continue its usual food expenditure and that the food purchased with the bonus will be an *addition* to the household's diet. If the purchase requirement is less than the household's former expenditure, some substitution of the bonus for the household's own expenditure is possible, and the amount of food consumption is increased by less than the full amount of the bonus.

For reasons discussed further in chapter four, it happens that the purchase requirement is higher than what many prospective food stamp participants are paying for food. To join the program,

---

[5] Grocers with a potential food stamp clientele apply readily for certification, redeeming the food stamps at their banks. Studies have indicated that food sales of retail grocery stores were up as much as 8 percent (after adjustment for seasonal variation) over sales reported prior to the introduction of the food stamp program. In addition, it was found that customers using food coupons spent considerably more per transaction than customers not using coupons, a procedure which has the potential to reduce business overhead costs.

therefore, they must shift some of their nonfood expenditures to the food category. Often most of their budget is already committed to fixed expenditures such as rent, utility, and installment payments. A shift of expenditures is practically impossible for them, and therefore they do not participate in the program.

The Education Gap

Lack of knowledge about nutrition in poor households is another factor restricting their response to diet improvement efforts. Since educational achievement is generally related to income level, the poor are more likely to be unaware of what "good nutrition" means. Some families do not participate in programs to improve their diet because they are unaware of the costs of poor nutrition. The government food programs have never had nutrition education components that would motivate poor families to participate. Sometimes welfare agencies offer nutrition education or homemaker programs, but in general these services have been especially inadequate for low-income families who require a different type of nutrition education than has been offered to the middle class.

Nutritionists and home economists, somewhat insecure about their status within the scientific disciplines, have been reluctant to abandon their technical discussions to take up the mundane problems of getting nutritious foods onto the tables of poor households. The concept of good nutrition appears to be second nature to most educated people who have long since forgotten where they learned about it, but individuals from poor families, who are likely to have had less than a high school education, may never have been taught that there is a relationship between the food they eat and the proper growth and development of their bodies. It may be a revolutionary idea to them that how they eat will affect their health and energies, now and in the future.

Dealing with low-income families takes more than the usual superficial public relations efforts of education programs directed at the entire population. One of the characteristics of poor fam-

35

ilies is that they do not participate in community activities as much as other families do. They do not attend cooking classes at the YWCA or open houses sponsored by the PTA. Reaching them requires personal visits and special incentives. Since professionals in nutrition have rarely been willing to undertake such a task, the sub-professional nutrition aide has come into being to provide a bridge between knowledge and culture.

The nutrition aide, usually indigenous to the neighborhood or income class, teaches low-income homemakers about adequate diets, purchasing, preparing, and serving food on a low budget, and is culturally attuned to motivate poor families to exert some effort to improve their diet.

To achieve an adequate diet with their lower food consumption, these low-income households would need to have more technical knowledge about nutrition than the average household possesses. They would have to make a conscious attempt to achieve an adequate diet, and they would have little margin for error. It is difficult, in fact, to say just how much conscious motivation to achieve an adequate diet there is in a middle-income household. The tastes and habits of these households stimulate them almost automatically to buy enough food to provide a margin of safety above a minimally adequate diet; knowledge and motivation probably are not consciously applied to the task. It is not likely, however, that those with poverty incomes will be able to buy the variety and quantity of food that would achieve for them, by chance, an adequate diet.

Freedom to Choose

Restricting the household's freedom to choose the composition of its diet will limit the effectiveness of a food program by discouraging participation or reducing the amount of free food that is ultimately consumed by participants. The recipient household in the commodity distribution program cannot choose the composition of the food supplement. This gives the food distributed in the

36

program a "poor man's" label, no matter what the items are or how high their quality.

Restricted choice is probably more keenly felt in food programs than in other types of welfare programs because we are all intensely involved emotionally with food. A nutrition sociologist explains why this is so.

[Food] is so vital to our very existence. We are very aware that if we do not eat and drink we are not going to stay alive for very long. Food is also one of the very first means by which we demonstrate our mood and individuality; thus a baby demands food and then perhaps rejects it; it asserts its personality by demanding particular foods and rejecting others. As we grow older, simply because we eat three meals a day, we come to regard ourselves as experts on the subject. In the same way, food asserts itself as an integral part of our culture and many social events in our lives take place round the meal table.[6]

Evidence that low income does restrict food choice is reflected in the fact that as income rises, households buy more meat, poultry, and fish and fewer cereal products, indicating that they prefer the former but that their low income has restricted them to foods which provide more bulk for the money spent.

Nutrition education specialists have recognized for years that diets can be improved only within the cultural framework of the society. Attempting to change food habits can only be successful if recommended innovations are consistent with the beliefs and attitudes of the target population in a way which goes beyond the question of food or nutrition. Recent developments in psychology have supported this theory for many types of persuasive communication.

Food has meaning for people which goes beyond its nutritional role. Sociologists have pointed out the social status implications of white bread and large quantities of sugar and have noted the reluctant acceptance in peacetime of foods which were first introduced as substitutes necessitated by war. To accord with cultural practices, nutritionists have been careful not to deprecate the

[6] John C. McKenzie, "Poverty: Food and Nutrition Indices," Office of Health Economics, London, 1967.

moral code of African tribes or to suggest two-o'clock feedings where there are no clocks, but within the United States, they have been slow to recognize cultural differentials. The programs directed to the low-income population have generally had many characteristics which aggravate the resentment low-income families already harbor because lack of choice is ubiquitous in their lives. The Nixon Administration recently undertook a comprehensive study in three southern states to find out if Americans who are poor can learn to eat a protein-rich food product that has been shipped to needy people abroad for years.[7] The success of such a project is problematical—and not because it has not been tried. A Department of Agriculture official testified before the Select Committee on Nutrition and Human Needs in 1968:

> You cannot develop a poor man's food, and make it practical. This has been tried. People have tried to take the cheapest way of making good nutrition, and give it to people as a way of solving the problem. But people, no matter how poor, no matter how hungry, have just as sophisticated tastes as the rest of us. They like things that taste well, and they like to eat things that other people who are not so poor eat.
>
> I will never forget a sign I saw in Jamaica . . . "You don't have to be a rich man to enjoy a drink that millionaires prefer" . . . an ad for Schweppes Bitter Lemon.[8]

In addition to motivational problems, there are very practical obstacles that develop when the household cannot choose the food items it prefers. The homemaker may not know how to cook the food available, either to make it acceptable to her family or to preserve its nutrient qualities. Even if she knows how to do these things, too much work may be involved. Prodigious amounts of baking may be necessary to convert large quantities of flour distributed in the program into some form acceptable to the family. The homemaker frequently must do this baking without electric mixers and temperature-controlled ovens.

[7] "Protein-Rich Food Studied as a Diet for Poor in South," *New York Times,* March 1, 1970, 1–31.

[8] U.S., Congress, Senate, *Nutrition and Human Needs, Hearings* before the Select Committee on Nutrition and Human Needs of the United States Senate, 90th Cong., 2d sess., December 1969, Part 1, p. 105.

It is not unheard of for families without other food to mix their free flour with water and eat paste, sometimes flavoring it with a little molasses, but these families usually have nothing else to eat. Experience with the commodity program has shown that households with anything else at all to eat will throw away any excess foods rather than eat them in an unpalatable form. Sometimes these foods are sold to "entrepreneurs" who buy it far below market price and resell it for a good profit. The recipient family that does not want the commodity is vulnerable to this illegal transaction, even at low compensation.

Nonmonetary costs

Finally, a household may refuse to take advantage of a diet-improvement opportunity if the nonfood or nonmonetary costs such as transportation and embarrassment offset the gain in food consumption. The importance of these factors to some participants is illustrated by the following testimony from a food stamp hearing:

> . . . Participants in the food stamp program do not have to suffer the indignity of waiting in a commodity line while some indifferent commissary clerk doles out their regular allotment of peanut butter and dried milk. The food stamp program contributes to the maintenance of self-respect by those whose pride and well-being have been impaired by the unhappy circumstances of poverty.[9]

Some food stamp program participants have complained that they are embarrassed because they are not allowed to tear the food stamps out of the coupon book and use them much the same as money. They say the procedure whereby the grocery clerk must tear the stamps out of the book (an attempt to eliminate illegal

[9] Statement of Joel Dressler, Committee for Miners and the Appalachian Committee for Full Employment in U.S., Congress, Senate, *Food Stamp Act of 1964, Hearings* before the Committee on Agriculture and Forestry, United States Senate, on H.R. 10222, 88th Cong., 2d sess., June 1964, p. 79.

transfer of coupons) makes it look as though they can't even calculate how many food stamps they need to pay for their groceries.

Some other elements in the design and administration of the federal family food programs which add to the nonfood and nonmonetary costs of participants are described in chapter four.

We can see from this discussion of the poor household's response to the federal food programs that the limitations of these programs are in large part attributable to the fact that they do not adequately take into consideration the factors that reduce the poor household's motivation to improve its diet. Their design has been influenced to a large degree by the fact that our society believes it is necessary to choose exactly how the poor should live, and this extends as far as to say what, as well as how much, they should eat.

It is a common opinion that any increased income received by the poor will be diverted from the food budget to nonfood needs, but empirical expenditure data generally contradict this hypothesis. The 1960–61 Bureau of Labor Statistics Consumer Expenditure Survey shows that the marginal propensity to consume food (the proportion of an income increase spent on food) is positive for all family types at low income levels. There is no evidence to indicate that poor households would not increase their consumption of food if their incomes rose.

In fact, there is evidence that the commonly accepted theory known to economists as Engel's law—that the proportion of income spent on food falls with rising income—may not be true for the lowest income levels. A British food expenditure survey gives some indication that the average propensity to consume food actually rises at the lowest levels until a minimally acceptable diet is reached, and this is consistent with food consumption data we have obtained from developing countries.[10]

We are unable to predict with certainty how poor households would allocate any increased income. The only data available on

[10] McKenzie, "Poverty."

food expenditures is cross-sectional—that is, obtained at one point in time from households classified over the income range. When this kind of data is used to predict how a household would behave when it moves from one income category to another over a period of time, one must assume that differences in food consumption between income levels at any one period of time represent changes which would occur if one household moved from one income level to another over a period of time. Changes in food expenditure that are due to economic and social factors other than income cannot be considered. But it might be true that the extent to which expenditures on food change with income are influenced more by social position, education, family stability, etc., than by the amount of the income change itself, and this would not show up in these data. Of course, since these factors do correlate to some extent with income, using cross-sectional data is probably not entirely misleading.

Another influence on the design of these programs is our keen desire to keep the poor from getting something for nothing. Therefore we make sure that the difficulty and embarrassment of participating in these programs is enough of a sacrifice that it will serve as a test that only the really needy will be willing to undergo.

The lack of participation in the food programs because of these restrictions that reduce the motivation of poor households to improve their diets defeats our objective of eliminating malnutrition, but we have apparently made this secondary to keeping the poor in their place.

4

The Food Programs: Only Half Trying

In 1935, Section 32 of the Agricultural Adjustment Act was amended to provide for the use of 30 percent of the customs receipts collected during each calendar year and unused balances up to $300 million for encouraging export and domestic consumption of agricultural commodities. In 1937 the commodity distribution program (sometimes known as the direct distribution or the surplus commodities program) was specifically authorized under Section 32 and continues to operate under this authority today. That it operates under Section 32 means that it is financed by an ongoing fund and does not require yearly appropriations by Congress. The Agricultural Act of 1949 (Section 416) and the Food and Agriculture Act of 1965 (Section 709) increased the food that was available for the program.

The average monthly participation in the commodity program was at a peak in 1939, when over 13 million persons were receiving $66 million (at market prices) worth of food, a little over $5 worth per person, on the average. This food, however, represented only a small part of the average yearly food consumption of persons on relief. Up to 1942, needy families were the largest recipients of Section 32 commodities. Immediately prior to World War II, a food stamp program (not the current program) began to replace the commodity program for poor families.

The early food stamp program at its peak served four million persons in 345 areas at a cost of $112 million in the year ending June 1942. The average bonus amounted to about $32 a year per person, compared with $5 worth of food distributed under the commodity program. It was abolished in 1943 when the war raised the demand for agricultural commodities and increased employment. From the time of the program's demise, there was a food stamp bill introduced in Congress every session until the current food stamp act was passed in 1964.

The present food stamp program, authorized by the Food Stamp Act of 1964, had its origins in a pilot program established in McDowell County, West Virginia, by Executive Order of President Kennedy in January 1961. The pilot programs were financed with Section 32 funds.

Additional pilot food stamp programs were inaugurated in eight economically depressed areas of the country in mid-1961. Each of these areas had been participating in the commodity program which was terminated when the food stamp program was introduced. By 1963 there were 43 pilot programs reaching 380,000 people. President Johnson signed the program into law on August 31, 1964, with appropriations voted through fiscal year 1967. By January 1967, there were 112 local food stamp projects in operation.

INADEQUATE SUPPLEMENTS

Participation in a government food program does not protect a poor family from hunger and malnutrition. Many households in these programs still have diet problems because neither of the programs has as its objective the provision of an adequate diet to every participating household. Both are designed to provide only a limited food supplement. Some families achieve an adequate diet with this limited supplement because they spend their own money for food up to the point at which the bonus stamps or free commodities can bring their total food consumption up to an adequate level. The very-low-income families who have little of their own money to spend on food do not get enough free food or stamps to

Table 4. Comparison of Value of Food Stamps Received with Cost of Low-Cost Food Plan

| | Low-cost Food Plan Monthly Expenditure | Food Stamp Program Purchase Requirement Schedule (South) | |
		Household Income	Purchase Requirement Plus Bonus
2-person family (ages 20–35)	$ 71.30	Under $20	$30
		$120–140	$42
4-person family (2 schoolchildren)	$120.30	Under $30	$58
		$130–150	$72
		$340–370	$102

SOURCE: U.S. Department of Agriculture, Food Stamp Purchase Requirement Schedule, Feb. 1, 1969; "Cost of Food at Home Estimated for Food Plans at Three Cost Levels, March 1968, U.S. Average."

achieve diet adequacy. Table 4 compares the purchase-requirement schedule expenditure and bonus with the expenditure called for by the Department of Agriculture's Low-cost Food Plan.

Although the food programs were initiated as relief to the needy consumer, their potential to bring the diet of participants up to an adequate level has been greatly reduced because they have been directed primarily to increasing total food consumption and only secondarily to helping poor households improve their diets. The operation of these programs has been facilitated and justified to Congress by the fact that they are complementary to the federal government's efforts to support agricultural markets. Their design was influenced primarily by the pressures of food-producing interests. Secretary Freeman testified in Senate hearings on the food stamp bill:

> After nearly 3 years of careful experimentation and study, we are convinced that the stamp program represents a better and more efficient means of channeling more of the abundance of American agriculture to families in economic need.[1]

He was emphasizing the fact that eating meat was a more efficient

[1] U.S., Congress, House, *Food Stamp Act of 1964, Report* together with Minority and Separate Views to accompany H.R. 10222, Report No. 1228, 88th Cong., 2d sess., 1964, p. 10.

way of reducing surplus grains (used for animal feed) than eating flour.

To accord with the objective of increasing food consumption, the department insisted that the amount of free food provided by these programs be limited to what would actually be new consumption. They reasoned that a limited food supplement would offer the only chance for a bona fide increase in consumption, since it could be assumed that all families already consume on the basis of their own expenditure a quantity of food that serves as the basic diet. Any food beyond a small supplement would simply be used as a substitute for food normally purchased by the household, and would not add to aggregate food consumption. The department claims that low-income households, even those with very inadequate diets, will not drastically change their food-nonfood consumption patterns, so that anything more than a small stamp bonus would be illegally diverted to nonfood uses.

Further, the department believes that providing the *basic* diet for households that cannot afford to buy any food at all should be the responsibility of traditional welfare and income maintenance programs (public assistance, social security, unemployment compensation, etc.). If the department provided the entire diet, it claims that households would, at its expense, use what should be their food budget to fill family needs left unsatisfied because of the deficiencies in other agencies' programs.

That this does happen was borne out by a survey in the Mississippi Delta where the commodity program is the primary source of assistance for many low-income families. These families attempt to live on the donated commodities and can use the money they save on food to purchase other necessities. The food programs in this case are serving as proxies for other needed welfare services in counties where such things as free medical care are not available and where welfare payments are grossly inadequate.

PROGRAMS CAN IMPROVE DIETS

Although the potential of the federal food programs does suffer from the limited supplement they offer, they have made significant contributions to the diets of poor households, indicating that some adjustment in the size of the supplements could improve the potential of the programs to eliminate malnutrition entirely.

It is especially important that the family orientation of the programs has been effective for reaching young children whom, as we have noted in chapter two, are the persons most vulnerable to damage from nutritional deficiencies. Preschool-age children are difficult to reach through institutions outside the family. The shortage of day-care centers for children from needy families and the fact that children under three (the most vulnerable group) are seldom taken into those that do exist restricts the number of children that can be reached through these institutions.

The family orientation has other advantages also. Meals are normally a family function, and the concepts associated with good nutrition are reinforced in the minds of all family members by their association with the familiar meal preparation and serving activities. These new ideas become more acceptable when they are part of functions which fit in with long-established family culture patterns.

Under the commodity program the Department of Agriculture donates food acquired through price-support and surplus-removal purchases to states (and territories) for free distribution to needy families. This food is donated to the agency the governor designates as responsible for establishing the eligibility of potential recipients, usually the local department of public welfare. All costs of the program after the initial delivery of food to the state's designated agency, including the costs of transportation, storage, distribution, and recipient certification, are borne by the state and/or local government.

The nutrition available to participants in the commodity program varies with the composition of the food "bundle" distributed. The bundle is limited to items purchased by the Department of Agriculture in its agricultural support programs. Transportation and storage problems prevent the program from handling perishable items like fluid milk, fresh meats, poultry items, and fresh fruits and vegetables.

47

There is no way to predict whether the food from the commodity program will improve the diet of the recipient household. If the donated commodities are added to the food already consumed by a family, the program helps to improve the household's diet, although it does not necessarily bring it up to an adequate level. If the family substitutes the program's commodities for food it formerly bought itself, the diet would not be substantially improved and may even become worse. The nutrient value of the donated food might be higher or lower than that of the food for which it is substituted. In spite of the fact that it is possible by substitution to convert the food bonus into an income supplement, the Agriculture Department estimates that the food consumption of participants in this program actually does increase. This is one of the few times that a department estimate about the success of the food programs has probably been an understatement. The commodity program has probably saved a good many families from starvation. A witness at the poverty subcommittee hearings in Jackson, Mississippi, described how "the surplus commodities got the people through last winter."[2] Many destitute families live almost solely on commodities.

In 1960 the value of the market basket in the commodity program fell to $1.20. Over 200 counties dropped out of the program, complaining that the value of the donated food was not worth the administrative costs of storing and distributing it. In an attempt to raise the food and monetary value of the programs, the department subsequently added a number of commodities to the bundle. The monthly value of food distributed in the summer of 1967 was about $5.50 per person.

Under pressure from the "hunger" notoriety, the department increased the number of commodities in the program twice in 1968, and at the present time 22 commodities are being distributed. Only about 20 percent of participating counties distribute all of

[2] U.S., Congress, Senate, *Poverty Hunger and Federal Food Programs*, Subcommittee on Employment, Manpower, and Poverty of the Committee on Labor and Public Welfare, United States Senate, 90th Cong., 1st sess., July 1967, p. 4.

the commodities. Expense, lack of storage facilities, and lack of demand are the major factors restricting the number of products distributed in local programs. The average number of items distributed is about 17. Many programs distribute less. The commodities being offered are: flour, canned chopped meat, canned vegetables, fruit and vegetable juice, lard/shortening, evaporated milk, rice, non-fat dry milk, oats/wheat, peanut butter, egg mix, cheese, raisins/prunes, dehydrated potatoes, corn syrup, cornmeal, butter/margarine, dry beans, canned poultry meat, dry peas, corn grits, bulgur.

The department estimates that the full package can provide 79 percent of the NRC recommended allowance of calories, 140 percent of protein, 134 percent of calcium, 112 percent of iron, 136 percent of Vitamin A, 129 percent of thiamine, 146 percent of riboflavin, and 91 percent of Vitamin C. The criticism that these percentages probably assume a more perfect utilization of the food than is actually effected has been countered with the argument that the NRC standards upon which they are based may be higher than necessary to maintain health, implying, it appears, that in this program the poor have an even chance!

If the poor are too poor, they don't have any chance to improve their diet by means of the food stamp program because they will not be able to afford the minimum required to buy the stamps (50 cents a person up to a family maximum of $3). For those who can participate, however, the food stamp program can make a significant contribution to their diet. For those participants at the bottom of the income range the bonus can be many times what they pay for stamps. For those households approaching the top of the eligibility category, the bonus falls to as little as 19 percent. Table 5 is a representative portion of the Purchase Requirement Schedule.

A before-and-after survey showed that families participating in the food stamp program consumed food that was greater in both nutritional quality and money value than what they had consumed before. The participating families did not spend their stamps for luxury items. More than 80 percent of their increased consump-

Table 5. Schedule of Food Stamp Program Showing Purchase Price and Bonus, February 1, 1969—Southern Schedule

Monthly Net Income	Purchase Price	Bonus	Total
Two-person Household			
$0–19.99	$1	$29	$30
20–29.99	4	26	30
30–39.99	8	24	32
40–49.99	12	22	34
50–59.99	16	20	36
60–69.99	20	18	38
70–79.99	24	16	40
80–99.99	28	16	44
100–119.99	32	16	48
120–139.99	36	14	50
140 & over	40	12	52
Five-person Household [a]			
0–19.99	$2.50	$65.50	$68
40–49.99	16	56	72
80–89.99	38	44	82
120–129.99	54	40	94
160–179.99	64	34	98
200–219.99	72	30	102
240–259.99	80	28	108
280–299.99	88	28	116
330–359.99	96	28	124
420–449.99	108	28	136
480–509.99[b]	116	28	144

[a] Complete schedule for 5-person household not shown.

[b] Add $4 to monthly purchase price for each $30 of monthly income (or portion thereof) over maximum income shown on schedule.

SOURCE: U.S. Department of Agriculture, Marketing and Consumer Service.

tion (money value) was for animal products and fruits and vegetables. The increase in meat represented a rise in the quantity of meat consumed, not a shift to more expensive meat. The rise in the money value of dairy products, however, represented in part the substitution of fluid whole milk for the less expensive nonfat dry milk solids previously available in the commodity program.

Many congressmen prefer the commodity distribution program because it uses surplus foods. The irony is that it is possible that the substitution effect in this program could reduce or prevent any gain in food consumption. Free surplus commodities may reduce market purchases of food by the recipients, or part of the surplus commodities may be resold, competing with the portion of that commodity in the market. Either way, the market could be slightly depressed and the nutritional objectives of the program partially defeated. On the other hand, the provision in the food stamp program that requires the household to invest an amount equal to its normal average expenditure for food in order to get its bonus stamps prevents most families in this program from diverting their free food to nonfood uses. Bonus stamps are intended to provide a true supplement to the family diet. Studies have shown, in fact, that most of the bonus is spent for *additional* food.[3]

It should be noted that avoiding any significant substitution effect in the food stamp program requires the voluntary compliance of participants and grocers, for the provisions directed to eliminating the substitution effect could be vitiated if recipients sold their coupons or store owners allowed recipients to purchase nonfood items.

REACHING THE POOR

In addition to their limited potential for improving the diet of participating households, the food programs are designed and administered in such a way that many needy households never get the chance to participate.

Food programs are instituted on the basis of a state request. Participation in the program is voluntary, and upon the request of the governor, any state agreeing to abide by program standards may participate.

Usually a commodity program, financed from the earmarked Section 32 funds, can be instituted immediately, but the com-

[3] U.S. Department of Agriculture, *Food Consumption and Dietary Levels under the Pilot Food Stamp Program, Detroit, Michigan, and Fayette County, Pennsylvania*, Agricultural Economic Report No. 9 (Washington: Government Printing Office, 1962), p. 13.

munity has to be put on a waiting list for the food stamp program until funds for expansion are appropriated by Congress. If a state wants a program in several areas, it submits a priority listing, but the law does not require that the priority be based on need in terms of either the proportion or the absolute number of poor people in the community. It requires only that the department give "equitable treatment" to all states in relation to their relative need as determined by average income data and their willingness to assume the required share of administration costs.

Despite the fact that the Department of Agriculture for many years received more requests than it could satisfy, it did not establish programs solely on the basis of need. The department was unwilling to promote on its own initiative the establishment of programs in counties where the need was relatively greatest. Sometimes it followed the policy of establishing new programs in counties contiguous to areas with an already existing program so that administrative offices could serve a wider area. This method of expansion often left poor counties without programs while less needy counties had them, and the situation perpetuated itself in areas where rich and poor counties exist in clusters, as they do in the southeastern states. The department claimed that it was politically strategic to establish the program first in places where it could be assured of good administration, the lowest possible administrative costs, and effective results, in order to present the program in a favorable light to other communities and to the Congress.

In 1966 the Office of Economic Opportunity financed nearly $3 million of local administrative costs in selected areas of seven states in order to get food programs established there. Under pressure from OEO and the Senate Poverty Subcommittee, the Department of Agriculture in July 1967 began a project designed to insure that a food assistance program would be available in each of the thousand counties with the lowest per capita income.

As of January 1970, the food programs were operating in 2,731 of the 3,049 counties in the country and in 25 independent cities. The department was assisting 187 of these projects with administrative costs. In 38 areas it has undertaken direct administration of the program.

A community does not have to accept a food program, even if the Department of Agriculture agrees to pay the administrative expenses. Although the department can operate a commodity program without working through local authorities, it must use local storage and distribution facilities, which can make direct administration an awkward procedure without official cooperation. Actually, the food stamp program would be easier to administer directly, but the department has interpreted food stamp legislation and congressional committee reports to mean that it is forbidden to operate that program directly.[4] At any rate, the department's policy leans away from forcing programs upon communities, which is what direct administration amounts to. The success of such a program is questionable where recipients can be intimidated by local authorities not to participate.

MANY POOR EXCLUDED

Where food programs exist, many of the poor families are not eligible for them. The eligibility standards for needy families are those used in each state's federal-state public assistance program or are modifications of public assistance income standards which permit the deduction from gross family income of employment expenses (including child care), heavy medical expenses, and any rent paid that exceeds a certain proportion of family income.

The Department of Agriculture claims as a general rule that only the income–liquid-asset standards of public assistance are relevant for food program eligibility. However, many areas do apply additional regulations, such as residence requirements, so that very poor, newly arrived families who cannot qualify for public assistance, also get no help from the food programs.

[4] "Statement by Honorable Orville L. Freeman, Secretary of Agriculture before the House Committee on Education and Labor, Wednesday, May 28, 1968," p. 4.

Public assistance standards vary widely from state to state and are lower in most states than the poverty standards used by the federal government, so that many families with incomes below the official poverty line, but over public assistance standards, which may be as low as $175 a month for a family of four,[5] are not eligible for the food program that operates in their community.

The Department of Agriculture has justified excluding these poor households from the programs because a couple of studies have indicated that families with incomes near the maximum eligibility standard show little interest in participating in the food stamp program. The department was not surprised at this. For many years it operated on the theory that a family's willingness to participate in a program which, like the food stamp program, requires some investment of family income is a test of its true need. The fact that participation in the commodity program varied with the attractiveness of the bundle of free foods offered indicated, according to the department, that most of the families who participated in the program did not really need additional food, but used the commodities to free some of the income they formerly spent on food for other family needs.[6] The department considered this a waste of government funds.

The department also believed that the fall in participation rates when a county changed from the commodity to the food stamp program represented a completely voluntary action by eligible families because "they took themselves off the lists"—were not taken off by some government authority. Therefore, the department took no steps to increase the particularly low participation in the food stamp program.

Need to the department was represented not by the poor household that actually had an inadequate diet, but by the poor house-

[5] This is not the minimum public assistance *payment*. Many states set their maximum payments below their cost standard. A family of four with no other income may be receiving as little as $55 a month on public assistance.

[6] Don Paarlberg, *Subsidized Food Consumption* (Washington: American Enterprise Institute for Public Policy Research, 1963), p. 42.

54

hold which, *in the opinion of the department*, did not have the resources to purchase an adequate diet. The implication was that almost all low-income households could have an adequate diet if they spent a large enough portion of their income. The department failed to consider that shelter takes priority when it comes to the family budget. Surveys of public assistance recipients show that they often have to pay more than their maximum shelter allowance in order to get housing and consequently have less income available for other basic necessities.

The department also failed to recognize (or ignored) the fact that major problems in design and administration were reducing participation even by those who needed the food supplement badly.

In October 1969 the food programs were reaching about 7 million persons, 3.6 million in the commodity distribution program and 3.4 million in the food stamp program—about one-quarter of the poor.

LOCAL ADMINISTRATION

The Welfare Department

Institutions which are likely to discover a family's need for a more adequate diet and can motivate the family to exert some effort toward achieving one should serve as points of contact for the food programs. Institutions like schools, churches, and clinics can acquaint households with the benefits they can derive from participation in the program and help them with application procedures. Unfortunately, however, food program administration is usually restricted to the local welfare department.

The agricultural committees in Congress have traditionally shown some suspicion of any programs in the Department of Agriculture which have welfare objectives extending beyond the agricultural community. By assigning the job of determining eligibility in the food programs to the local welfare department, these legislators could assure their farm constituents that the free food would go only to those who could not afford to buy it and would therefore be used to increase total food consumption. Also they felt that this procedure would insure that the food programs would be handled according to community standards, trusting the local professional welfare establishment to defend from federal encroachment the community's traditional sovereignty over its own poor.

Most welfare departments appear to administer the food programs conscientiously within their ability to do so. Often, however, inadequate funds reduce their outreach activities, and participation in the food programs is limited by their inability to reach the poor families in their community who are not on welfare and frequently by the inability of the poor to reach them. Public assistance payments, the welfare department's raison d'être, are limited to certain categories of people within the poverty population, and probably no more than a third of the poor receive any welfare payments. Unless a family is on welfare, there is little occasion for it to come into contact with the welfare department; therefore, unless the welfare department is willing to undertake publicity and educational programs that reach into the whole poverty community, many of the poor will never know that a food program is available.

The "dole" connotation of programs emanating from the welfare department discourages some eligible families from applying for the food programs. Others are dismayed by the mountain of paper work and investigations involved in the means test. Some of them cannot afford to make the initial trip (or the two or three trips that might be required) to the welfare department to complete the negotiations necessary to establish eligibility.

Some welfare departments certify public assistance recipients from case records, making a trip to the welfare department unnecessary, but many welfare recipients, although they have an already-established contact with the department, must go to a lot of trouble to get certified. Procedures for those who are not welfare recipients—who have no contact with the welfare department and must weather the rigors of the means test—are even more involved.

Discrimination

Welfare department discrimination against minority groups in the community is not unknown. To keep the "undeserving" poor out of the food programs, welfare departments may put them off with an over-zealous application of the means test, unnecessarily complex regulations, and generally create minor but not necessarily illegal obstacles that scare and easily discourage people whose traditional mistreatment by the local establishment has made them unsure of their rights and reluctant to pursue the issue in the face of obvious establishment disapproval. When welfare departments discriminate in the administration of both the public assistance and the food programs, it often means that the very people who need the food supplement most, because they lack even minimum income support, do not participate in the food program.

There is evidence that in some communities the food programs have been used as a weapon of economic and political coercion and intimidation. For example, an all-white county board in a southern county withdrew its participation in the commodity program, in which participants were mostly Negro, as a reprisal against a voter registration drive. Food programs are discontinued during growing and harvest seasons in some areas to insure a hungry labor supply.

Delivery Problems

Commodity programs usually distribute food from one central warehouse on a limited number of days. Lack of manpower and funds prevents most counties from arranging several distribution points or mobile units. Isolated families without transportation and aged and disabled persons often have difficulty getting to the distribution center. Frequently families must pick up packages weighing well over a hundred pounds, and getting these bundles home is a constant problem.

In some places, transportation to the centers may be provided by the ubiquitous "entrepreneur," perhaps the owner of an old truck, who charges a fee and sometimes accepts part of the donated

57

food as payment. This reduces the benefits of the program to the needy family.

Some community antipoverty programs have used poverty or neighborhood aides to pick up and deliver commodities or stamps to immobile families or individuals, or to provide round-trip transportation for them when the county requires that the food be picked up in person.

PURCHASE REQUIREMENTS REDUCE PARTICIPATION

Participation rates in the food stamp program are much lower than those in the commodity program. There is no reliable estimate of what these rates are because variation in welfare standards and the lack of data on just how many nonwelfare families could become eligible makes it difficult to estimate the size of the eligible population. Participation rates in the commodity distribution program averaged about 85 percent in 1967. We would not be far wrong, I suspect, if we estimated an average participation rate in the food stamp program of 25 percent or less.

There is no doubt that the introduction of the food stamp program into a county that had a commodity program has resulted in large reductions in food program participation. Documented reductions in participation upon introduction of the food stamp program have varied from 18 to 85 percent. Washington County, Mississippi, showed a 50 percent reduction in food program participation when the county changed from the commodity to the food stamp program. In eight other counties in Mississippi that switched to stamps, participation dropped 36,000 persons during the first year.

The household's willingness to participate in the food stamp program depends on its ability to meet the purchase requirement. The family's income fluctuates with seasonal variations in employment and income, and so does its participation in the program. The fluctuating pattern of participation is more pronounced in rural areas where job opportunities are more seasonal.

A good case can be put forth to support the hypothesis that a major reason for lower participation rates in the food stamp program is that in some important respects, program design conflicts with the normal expenditure habits of the target population. Physical requirements and social standards compel even those with very inadequate diets to channel some of their expenditure to nonfood needs. The requirement that a significant amount of family income be invested each month in food stamps, perhaps much more than is currently being spent for food, may discourage eligible families from participating in the program.

The hypothesis that it is the required expenditure of household funds and not the idea of food stamps themselves that lead to low participation rates is indicated by the high rates of participation that were achieved in the early food stamp program that operated from 1939 to 1943.

The legislative authority of the first food stamp program was the same as that of the commodity program, Section 32 of the Agricultural Adjustment Act of 1935, and like that program, the early food stamp program was directed primarily at surplus disposal. The procedures for selling stamps were different from those used in the current program.

The early food stamp program required eligible families to invest $4 to receive $6 in stamps, regardless of income. The participation rates among eligible households reached 70 percent and higher in many areas.

Of course, the fact that the poverty population in the Depression included many well-educated, formerly middle-income people, accustomed to adequate diets, would account for some of the difference in participation levels between then and now. But further evidence that the difference in the required investment is crucial is the fact that participants in the early program could manipulate their food expenditures for stamps so that the stamps served as an income supplement as well as a food supplement. In fact, this is the reason the Department of Agriculture refused to renew the program after the war—department officials complained of the illegal use of coupons and of the diversion of surplus coupons to non-surplus foods, a practice which they estimated affected as much as one-quarter to one-third of the bonus stamps.

The participants in the current food stamp program have very little scope for using their stamps as an income supplement. A household of four persons with a monthly income of anywhere from $30 to $160 will have a purchase requirement that will amount to between 35 and 50 percent of its total income. Most purchase requirements are considerably above the estimated one-quarter to one-third that low-income families spend on food. Many eligible families feel they can get by with spending less than the purchase requirement, and, in fact, surveys have shown that many of them when participating in a program were spending more than they spent for food before they joined the program.

Nonparticipants commonly complain that food coupon costs are too high and that they are actually spending less than the purchase requirement. It has been noted in surveys, however, that some families are unaware of how much they spend for food, and many who complain that coupon costs are too high actually pay at least as much for food as they would in the program. These families often think they spend less than they do because the money dribbles out in day-to-day purchases that they do not keep track of. Some actually do spend less and do not recognize that their diet is inadequate.

The unrealistic aspects of the purchase requirements may be due to the fact that they were derived from surveys which were not representative of the "average" poor household's expenditures on food. For example, many poor families participating in the commodity program discontinue a large part of the expenditure they formerly made for food. When the food stamp program is established in their community, they are then not in the habit of spending an "average" amount for food. This probably accounts for much of the drop in participation when an area shifts from the commodity to the food stamp program. The purchase requirements do not reflect the new expenditure pattern and are set too high for the eligible population, whose expenditures for food drop below average. This oversight in the schedule is important because most of the present food stamp programs are in areas that formerly had commodity programs, and this will probably continue to be the case, since the Department of Agriculture expects eventually to replace all the commodity programs with new food stamp projects.

Some families participating in the food stamp program drop out of the program when their income increases because the proportion of new income that must be spent on food according to the purchase requirement schedule is unrealistic with respect to the family's relative demand for food and nonfood items. According to the present schedule, if a four-person household has an increase in its monthly income from $20 to $30, it must use 60 percent of this increase for food stamps. This is high compared to the typical proportion of new income spent on food in the low-income household which rarely goes above 30 percent. Further, if a family changes income categories by less than one dollar, it must still add to its purchase requirement the entire increase for that category. Thus, if the same household has an increase in its income from $28 to $30, it must still increase its expenditure for food stamps by $6. At the higher income levels, the marginal purchase requirements are less, but the "borderline" anomaly remains for all households. These high marginal increases in the purchase requirement schedule assume that poor families spend their new money for food first, but, as we have noted, when incomes rise above the survival level, the excess dollars in many instances are already fully committed.

In months when its income falls below the amount on which its purchase requirement was based, it is difficult for a family to make the required investment. Certification every month for families with fluctuating incomes is the ideal set forth by the Department of Agriculture, but most welfare departments do not have the resources to make a monthly certification, which often involves a personal visit to the family by a social worker.

Another major difficulty the potential participant faces is the accumulation of enough money to invest in the first month's supply of stamps. Regulations permit stamps to be sold as often as

61

once a week, but most areas do not have the resources to do this and limit their sales to once or twice a month. This can be a perpetual problem if, for example, the family's income comes in once a week, and food stamps require two or four weeks' investment in advance. To help relieve part of this problem, the Department of Agriculture in the latter part of 1967 permitted a first-month reduction of the purchase requirement for families that could not accumulate enough for the first month's full purchase requirement.

In defending the adequacy of his food allowance, the head of the Chicago Department of Public Aid said that since a family spending 80 percent of its food budget can get a 27 percent bonus in food stamps, and since only one-third of welfare recipients were taking advantage of this, he assumed that the others don't spend even 80 percent of their food allowance for food. He failed to recognize that a family has to spend 80 percent of its food allowance *at one time* to get the bonus, and many of the welfare recipients said they do not participate in the program because they do not want to give up that 80 percent at the beginning of the month in case an emergency arises later.

Since a minimum expenditure is necessary to buy stamps, families without income cannot participate in the food stamp program at all. The commodity program and the food stamp program are not operated concurrently in the same community (according to a provision in the Food Stamp Act), so that extremely poor families in the food stamp areas have no program available to them.

Until recently the minimum expenditure required for stamps was $2 a month per person (up to a maximum of $12 per family). The Department of Agriculture was pressured during the hunger crisis to reduce the minimum expenditure for families with monthly incomes up to $20 to 50 cents a person (with a maximum of $3 per family). The department asked local government authorities or welfare agencies to pay the 50-cent minimum purchase requirement when a family could not do so. Apparently administrative considerations were preventing the department from reducing the minimum to zero, even for families with no income.

President Nixon, shortly after he came into office, announced that food stamps would be issued free to those without income. At the present time this program provision is in operation in two counties in South Carolina.

Negro leader A. Philip Randolph told the National Advisory Commission on Rural Poverty that "government administrators seem not to understand that the poorest people simply don't have money" and live in a primitive world of barter. They work to pay off past debts or to establish future credit and simply do not participate in America's favorite pastime—buying.

5

The Total Responsibility: Hunger and Poverty

Who is to blame for the continued presence of hunger and malnutrition in the United States? The efforts to improve the diet of needy households have been hindered by the reluctance of Congress to support effective food programs for the poor, the Department of Agriculture's passive acceptance of Congress' lukewarm approach, and the half-hearted and unimaginative efforts with which it carried out program administration to meet the needs of the poor.[1]

In 1970, six years after initiation of the federal "War on Poverty" and four years after the "discovery" of hunger in Mississippi, major changes are only now being considered in food program policy. A few minor alterations were undertaken in the purchase requirement schedule after pressure was put on the department by the Senate Poverty Subcommittee's hearings and personally by influential members of Congress.

CONGRESSIONAL DISAPPROVAL

The members of the congressional agricultural appropriations committees do not fully approve of the federal food programs be-

---

[1] This criticism is directed to the policy-making levels in the department and not to the operating levels, which have administered the food programs conscientiously, with fewer resources than they needed.

cause these congressmen are primarily interested in the votes of their farm constituency. A food program that goes beyond an obvious surplus disposal program is in their eyes a welfare program which belongs in another agency, and a program which is taking funds away from the farmer, the rightful recipient of all funds appropriated for the Department of Agriculture.

In hearings held in June 1963 on the food stamp bill, Representative Charles Hoeven related his surprise that the Secretary of Agriculture would support a welfare program of only indirect benefit to farmers which would be charged entirely to the Department of Agriculture. Representative Hoeven suggested that the bill might more appropriately be administered by the Department of Health, Education, and Welfare.

The dialogue at Appropriations Committee hearings indicates the typical committee member's attitude toward such programs:

Senator Holland: In the case of an appropriation of this kind, you run right square into the policy of this committee frequently expressed that we do not permit agriculture to be charged with expenditures which have no relation to the support of agriculture.

Here you are asking for $195 million to be appropriated out of an earmarked fund [Section 32] for welfare purposes. It would be very hard to even persuade the general public or anybody else that that $195 million had not gone to the farmers of this country. . . .

Senator Young: If you start using these funds for other purposes, one day you won't have enough money in this fund to help protect perishable commodities which I have always felt should receive this benefit . . .[2]

In the report on the extension of the Food Stamp Act in 1967:

The present Food Stamp Program is rapidly growing toward a nationwide Federal welfare activity which is structured in an inefficient manner that is progressively destroying State and local responsibility while doing next to nothing for the benefit of American agriculture. . . .[3]

[2] U.S., Congress, Senate, *Department of Agriculture and Related Agencies Appropriations Hearings, Fiscal Year 1968*, H.R. 10509, 90th Cong., 1st sess., Part 1, p. 102; also see exchange, p. 481.

[3] U.S., Congress, House, *Food Stamp Program, Report together with Individual Views and Minority Report to accompany H.R. 1318*, Com-

The food stamp bill almost did not get out of committee in 1964, in spite of the fact that President Johnson had put it on his priority list of legislation. In June of that year, the House Committee on Agriculture held hearings on an administration bill to expand and make permanent the food stamp program, which up to that time had been a limited pilot effort supported by Section 32 funds. In February 1964, the Agriculture Committee voted 19–14 to table the bill. One month later, however, the vote was reversed when several southern Democrats changed their vote in return for potential support by northern Democrats on a pending tobacco bill. The bill passed the House on the basis of a log-rolling arrangement with the supporters of the Cotton-Wheat bill.

In Senate hearings the committee members objected that the program's guidelines were not strong enough to prevent ineligible families from participating and that since the states actually contributed very little money to the program, they would have no incentive to keep ineligible recipients out. The food stamp program seemed extremely expensive when compared with the commodity program's less costly distribution of an already-purchased surplus.

In 1967 when the Food Stamp Act was renewed for another two years, an amendment requiring states to pay 20 percent of the cost of programs in their state, a provision which would have crippled the program in the areas where it is most needed, was defeated in the House by a narrow 18-vote margin.

Since the food supplement programs would not, even if they were expanded to fill the total food gap of the poor, make a significant contribution to reducing the agricultural surplus, it is unlikely that these congressional attitudes toward the food programs will change.

BUREAUCRATIC LETHARGY

Characteristic of the department's half-hearted efforts to improve the food programs is that when the department was pres-

mittee on Agriculture, U.S. House of Representatives, 90th Cong., 1st sess., April 1967, p. 12.

sured into reducing the price of food stamps for people with little or no income, it reduced it from $2 a person to 50 cents a person for the income range $0–9.99 ($0–19.99 in the south), but the price of stamps for a family with an income of $10 remained at $2 per person. The department never gave a satisfactory explanation of why it could not reduce the price to zero for those with no income, especially in view of the fact that it was not making any food available through other programs to destitute families in food stamp areas. Secretary Freeman pointed out that these families had to be eating something or they would not be alive. That meant that since somebody was spending money on food for them, it was not necessary for the department to furnish their whole diet (that is, give them free food stamps), even if they had no money of their own.

Lack of imaginative administration was demonstrated in a number of areas. Secretary Freeman invoked economic constraints as the reason for slow progress in expanding food programs, but the department had never requested for the food programs substantially more funds than it had received. Some time afterward, Freeman did ask Congress to expand the food stamp program significantly.

The legal constraints which Freeman at various times said prevented him from improving the programs were not insurmountable. After refusing to authorize emergency action in Mississippi,[4] he admitted the possibility of carrying on a food program under emergency conditions if "he were convinced there were a number of hungry people in that county."[5] He went on to indicate his reluctance to take such a step.

[4] The Food Stamp Act (Sec. 4b) prohibits distribution of federally-owned food under any law "except during emergency situations caused by a national or other disaster as determined by the Secretary." The General Counsel of the Senate Subcommittee on Employment, Manpower, and Poverty sent a memorandum to the Secretary of Agriculture stating that a reasonable interpretation of the legislative history of the Food Stamp Act would permit the secretary to undertake emergency food distribution in the Mississippi hunger crisis. Apparently the General Counsel at the Department of Agriculture disagreed.

[5] U.S., Congress, Senate, *Hunger and Malnutrition in America, Hearings*

There is no doubt that with the resources available to it, both monetary and technical, the department could have programmed an adequate diet consisting of products selling below 90 percent of parity (for which Section 32 funds can be legally spent) and adjusted it from month to month to meet the dietary deficiencies of the poor, as well as price-support objectives, at the very least in emergency situations. That this potential did exist is clearly evidenced by recent extensive expansion of the list of foods offered in the commodity program.

The accounting system used by the executive branch discourages the Department of Agriculture from taking steps to remedy the obvious problems of the food programs. The narrow view engendered by budget practices has not been broadened by the institution of the Planning, Programming, Budgeting System (PPBS). Under this system each agency establishes priorities for all its programs, including poverty programs, in terms of its own objectives. Major inter-agency coordinating decisions concerning the whole federal poverty effort are made within the executive branch by the Bureau of the Budget with the help of the Office of Economic Opportunity, which has some government-wide coordinating and planning responsibilities in the poverty area.

The ultimate objective of the Budget Bureau analysis is the most efficient government-wide allocation of resources to alleviate and eliminate poverty. The pursuit of this objective calls for trade-offs within and among agencies; however, because PPBS is a new operation, because the traditional budget analysis (which tends to downplay the role of objectives in the planning function) is still quite firmly entrenched within the agencies, and because vested interests for certain programs naturally develop in any agency, the new system works more effectively for intra-agency than for inter-agency allocation. The potential of the food programs to improve the diet of the poor and to complement overall antipoverty objectives has been hindered by the inability of PPBS to provide effec-

---

before the Subcommittee on Employment, Manpower, and Poverty of the Committee on Labor and Public Welfare, United States Senate, 90th Cong, 1st sess., July 1967, pp. 138.

tively for a reallocation of antipoverty resources across agency lines.

From the government's point of view, what is spent on expanding programs for the poor in one area can save on antipoverty expenditures in other areas. However, this saving does not necessarily materialize for an individual agency. If the Department of Agriculture broadened its food programs beyond the participants' present food gap, it would be financing to some extent, depending on the amount of substitution of nonfood for former food expenditure, the needs of poor households that are normally the responsibility of other agencies.

In view of this, it is not difficult to understand why the department has been reluctant either to increase the target population of the food programs or to increase the amount of the food supplements. First, the department has not traditionally had any general welfare objectives that go beyond the agricultural community. Second, expanding the program under such circumstances is not a rational alternative for the department in terms of conserving its own resources because it has no other antipoverty programs on which it could save. And finally, expanded food programs would not significantly contribute to other department objectives, such as increasing the demand for food.

The Department of Agriculture's need to maintain good relations with local leaders and farmers whose cooperation is needed in agricultural support programs discourages it from taking aggressive action at the local level. Welfare is often a controversial issue in the community, and the department is reluctant to risk the effectiveness of its major agricultural and rural development programs by pushing a food program on a community against the wishes of its influential inhabitants.

THE PUNITIVE WELFARE SYNDROME

Secretary Freeman pointed out in one of his hunger crisis statements that "public awareness and public support of our effort to feed the hungry are two commodities that have been in short supply over the past seven years." Although this is true, the department did not hold up its end of what must be a cooperative effort on the part of the bureaucracy and the public by keeping the public informed about the issues. The truth is that the department's inability to recognize its own punitive attitudes toward the poor limited its insight into the problems involved in improving their diet. One probably would not be far from wrong in saying that the department did not even know there was a problem.

It is interesting to note as an example of the punitive welfare attitudes inherent in the department's food program policies Secretary Freeman's remarks in a department publication about the "success" of the food stamp program:

The program since 1961 has been uniquely successful; no major scandal has developed in its operation. Strong supervisory, audit and investigatory procedures are constantly under way . . .[6]

These remarks reflect the ever-present suspicions of "give-away" programs rather than the substantial improvement which the program has made in the diets of many poor households.

The punitive welfare syndrome was not, however, invented by the Department of Agriculture. Traditionally, communities have classified their own poor into "deserving" and "undeserving" categories, using a standard that combined the Protestant Ethic and the sexual code of the Victorian era. The "deserving" were worthy of being helped by public welfare programs which provided them with whatever the community believed they needed. We have noted that the department had a similar view. It believed that many of the poor have inadequate diets because they will not, not because they cannot, spend enough for food; therefore, they are not deserving of help.

This view is representative of the attitudes which our whole society has held toward the poor for hundreds of years. It has only been within the past few years that as a society we have for

[6] U.S. Department of Agriculture, "Food—Hunger: 1968," Press Release, May 21, 1968, p. 4.

71

government policy purposes been willing to define the target population of public poverty programs solely on the basis of need, measured by an income rather than by a moral standard. According to the economic opportunity philosophy, the income of the poor is low because imperfections in the allocation of resources have denied to them the same opportunities to earn adequate incomes that most people in the United States automatically receive. It is not possible to classify anyone as "undeserving" until he has been given an equal chance to earn his own way.

Although the Department of Agriculture is very likely to be right in line with the welfare philosophy of many communities upon whom it must depend to run the food programs, it has been a few years behind the times according to federal poverty criteria.

THE ALLOCATIVE DECISION

Since the federal government has declared its intention to eliminate the causes of poverty in the United States, it does not matter whether participants in food programs need the food itself or need it to free income for other necessities. The significance of any diversion of resources in poor households is that the family does not have enough to cover all of its needs. It is only incidental that food needs, because they appear to be more flexible than other needs, are found to be satisfied less adequately under these circumstances. In terms of an efficient allocation of federal government resources aimed at the elimination of poverty, whether the diet of the poor should be improved by increasing the scope of the food programs, by providing more and better housing, by expanding medical services, or by increasing money payments, etc., would depend solely on the cost-effectiveness of each of the many individual programs and various combinations of them with respect to diet-improvement and other antipoverty objectives.

The economic opportunity philosophy espouses the idea that the major difference between the poor and nonpoor is the extent to which each is free to choose the material and cultural components of his environment. The poor are different from the nonpoor because their choice of living standards is restricted, not because they innately prefer different standards. The problem of poverty can be solved by providing the poor with opportunities to improve their income-earning abilities, which would be the first step toward enlarging their choices. It is not necessary or desirable to choose their standards for them. In accord with this definition of poverty, programs undertaken to alleviate the symptoms of poverty should provide income, not specific goods and services. This method has the further advantage of making the poor less distinguishable from the nonpoor.

Thus, efficiency and philosophy support the idea that in-kind programs are an inappropriate method of helping low-income households to improve their living standard.

Raising income in accordance with the economic opportunity philosophy by means of economic growth, education, and employment training takes a long time to produce results for individual households, and an adequate income maintenance program for all families who need it is too controversial for immediate enactment. It will, therefore, be some time before the income of the poor is raised by these means. Because economic opportunity programs are not capable of *immediately* attacking the problem of inadequate diet, and because the poor may lack the motivation or knowledge to obtain a fully adequate diet, either with or without more income, it could be argued that even though food programs restrict freedom of choice, they are necessary as stop-gap measures to save young children from permanent physical and mental damage and to provide older children and adults with diets which give them the best chance for remaining healthy, alert people. The dangers of malnutrition may justify the temporary restriction of choice as a means to insure that recipients are healthy enough to take advantage of programs aimed at permanently improving their opportunities to choose.

A food program, then, would be acceptable to maintain minimum diet standards in the short-run, but we must recognize a significant distinction here. The food program should no longer be an attempt to dictate a life style—that such-and-such a percentage

73

of poor households' expenditures should be for food. It is a substitute for an immediate income increase that we find impossible to bring about in some more preferable way. Therefore, the major objective of the food program should be to achieve the participation of all needy households, whether or not some of them ultimately use part of their food to free some of their income for nonfood needs. In other words, it is necessary to sacrifice some of the program's efficiency to increase food consumption in return for increasing its ability to eliminate some of the elements of poverty, whether or not they are related to food consumption.

FOOD PROGRAM REFORM

The flexibility of the food stamp program gives it the potential to achieve diet adequacy and high rates of participation with adjustments in the bonus and purchase requirements. In order to assure that all needy families can participate and can achieve an adequate diet, a food stamp program with the following changes should be made the country's major family food distribution program:

The bonus (number of free stamps) should be raised to permit all participating households to obtain an adequate diet with their stamps.

The purchase requirement schedule should be adjusted to take into consideration the target population's actual expenditure habits, including their income elasticity of demand for food and nonfood items and whether the potential recipient has been participating in another food program which would have enabled him to reduce his food expenditures below the "normal" amount.

There should be provision for emergency recertification and reestablishment of a household's purchase requirement when income changes.

Loans should be available to permit the purchase of stamps by households whose "pay-days" do not coincide conveniently with the food stamp issuance day and for participants who have an emergency that requires cash when a large part of their income is invested in food stamps.

Uniform federal standards of eligibility should be established for all food stamp projects based on the official poverty lines.

The federal government should pay administrative costs of the program in counties which cannot afford to pay such costs.

The federal government should operate the program directly when a need can be established and the community refuses to operate a program.

Eligibility procedures should require only a simple application containing a sworn statement as to household income and assets, and these applications should be made available in schools, clinics, hospitals, community centers, churches, and other places that are normal contacts for low-income families and should be processable by mail.

An educational component using indigenous aides when possible to inform the target population about the existence of the program, the procedures for applying, and the benefits and constituents of an adequate diet, should be made an integral part of the program in all communities. Such services should be made available only to those who want them, should not be a condition of participation in the program, and should be in addition to the provision of an adequate diet, not a substitute for an inadequate bonus.

While a food stamp program with the above changes can meet the food needs of the poor, the responsibility to eliminate poverty which we as a society have taken upon ourselves requires that we meet the needs of such households with a more comprehensive program that can immediately give them, in addition to a fully adequate diet, any other services required to raise their standard of living to an acceptable level. In the long run all subsidies to low-income households should take the form of a cash payment that would assure an acceptable psychic as well as physical living standard.

To facilitate the development of viable alternatives for improving the diet of low-income households, the family food programs should be operated by an agency which has the major responsibility for other types of family income maintenance and service programs. Under these circumstances alternatives to the food programs can be analyzed more easily in terms of both nutrition and antipoverty objectives.

In order to assure an ultimate allocation of diet-improvement resources that complements general poverty objectives, the family food programs should be transferred from the Department of

Agriculture to the Department of Health, Education, and Welfare, where resource allocation can be analyzed for operational purposes as a part of the broad spectrum of other welfare programs operated by that agency. Such a move would allow a more systematic review of costs and benefits of food programs to be developed, since alternatives for achieving the same objective are already part of HEW's activities.

HEW could directly relate any improvements it made in the food programs to savings and/or objectives in some of its other programs. Although these improvements might raise the cost of the food programs, the agency would still have an incentive to effect them. The Department of Agriculture is less motivated to meet general welfare objectives and, at the same time, has less incentive to do so because it risks reducing the effectiveness of its other programs.

It is clear that legislative and/or administrative changes alone cannot make a food supplement program fully effective in raising the dietary levels of the needy in the face of inadequate income for other necessities. Without adequate income, there will be a tendency for the recipients either to substitute the free foods for their former food purchases in order to increase their purchase of other family necessities or a reluctance of eligible households to participate in any food program which requires a fixed investment in food and hampers their ability to adjust expenditures to meet other family needs. If our objective is to dictate a food consumption increase, we have lost nothing by their failure to participate; but if we established the program because we could not afford economically or morally the loss of human resources that fall victim to malnutrition, then we are only successful if our program has a high rate of participation.

The transfer to HEW could bring into active participation many agencies within the department whose programs in local communities could be used as a contact point for the food program. Agencies sponsored by the Public Health Service, the Office of Child Development, the Social and Rehabilitation Service, and the Office of Education could establish outreach facilities in such places as clinics, day-care centers, training programs, and schools to increase program participation throughout the needy population.

Welfare economists argue that subsidizing only food consumption does not yield maximum consumer satisfaction and that a more effective way would be to grant general income or price concessions to consumers so that they could satisfy all tastes and preferences and not be forced to allocate their subsidy for just one group of commodities. Placing the food programs in an agency which handles the bulk of the government welfare programs would indicate more clearly that the effectiveness of the family food programs in improving diets depends on a family's ability to meet all of its needs and should lead eventually to a decision that any increase in resources needed to satisfy nutrition and other poverty objectives should be directed toward programs that insure some minimum level of cash income. Because we cannot separate nutrition from antipoverty objectives when either freedom of choice or the technical problems of achieving an adequate diet are considered, there is some question about the efficiency of allocating resources to food programs rather than to cash income payments. This question is unlikely to be posed under the current allocation of administrative responsibilities.

In the long run, it is hoped that the transfer of the food program responsibilities to HEW would lead to the elimination of food programs completely and to the provision of "food" subsidies through income maintenance programs designed to attack the total poverty problem.

6

The Next Step

In fiscal year 1969, the Department of Agriculture spent about $470 million on the two family food programs. The value of food distributed in the commodity program was $224.9 million, and the value of bonus coupons and the federal administrative expenses in the food stamp program was $238.6 million. (The major administrative expenses of the commodity program are paid by state and local governments and data are not available on these costs.)

In fiscal 1970, the department used an increased appropriation totaling $610 million to expand the food stamp program into new areas and to make some minor modifications in the purchase requirement schedule. The department has acknowledged the need for substantially reducing the participants' cash payments for coupons and for providing a total coupon allotment for all households that will be sufficient to provide a nutritionally adequate diet. Food stamp legislation now before Congress contains provisions for these changes, and the department's fiscal 1971 budget estimate for the program of $1.3 billion is based on passage of this legislation. The department anticipates that a participation level of 5.4 million people will be reached in the food stamp program by June 30, 1970, and that with the expanded funds in fiscal 1971, 7.5 million persons will be served under a much more adequate food stamp program.

The cost of filling the food gap of all poor households has been estimated to be as much as $4 billion. Generally these estimates are based on the cost of food needed to bring each poor household's diet up to an adequate level. If the present food stamp program were used to fill the food gap for all the poor, this method of estimating costs would be reasonable, as there is little scope for substituting nonfood for food needs in the program as it is presently designed. However, proposed legislation calling for an expansion of the food stamp program to the total poor population includes provisions that would give poor families wide scope for substituting free food for former food expenditures and therefore for using the program as an income supplement. The diets of many participants in such a program might remain inadequate, and increased program expenditures would be necessary to achieve diet objectives. The costs of a food program that serves as an income supplement should, therefore, not be based on the food gap but on the poverty gap. The present poverty gap is estimated to be almost $10 billion. The size of the poverty gap might be affected by the food program itself if its income supplement potential influenced work incentives.

Adequate cash income programs for families below the poverty line would reduce the cost of food programs and could even make food programs unnecessary. At the present time, there is no program to provide cash income to poor households simply because they are needy. Certain poor households, where the head is blind, totally disabled, or over 65, and those with children where there is no male head, are eligible for payments under the present federal-state public assistance programs. However, not even all poor households in these categories are eligible because most states have income standards in these programs that are below the official poverty lines. The inadequate payments and coverage provided by these programs has been almost universally acknowledged.

80

Although a few families with unemployed male heads receive help from a special public assistance program available in only a few states, for the most part poor families with employable male heads, working or unemployed, are not eligible for assistance, no matter how desperate their economic situation. The Family Assistance Plan proposed by President Nixon to replace Aid to Families with Dependent Children would make all families with children, even those with working male heads, eligible for assistance on the basis of income standards shown in Table 6. An assured $1600 minimum for a family of four would be available to every family with children whose income is below this amount. The family could earn $720 in additional income with no reduction of the

Table 6. Family Assistance Plan Proposed Federal Guarantee*

Family Size	Minimum Guarantee	Earnings	Assistance Payments	Total Income
2	$1,000	$ 720	$1,000	$1,720
	1,000	1,500	610	2,110
	1,000	2,000	360	2,360
	1,000	2,720	0	2,720
3	1,300	720	1,300	2,020
	1,300	1,500	910	2,410
	1,300	2,500	410	2,910
	1,300	3,320	0	3,320
4	1,600	720	1,600	2,320
	1,600	1,500	1,210	2,710
	1,600	3,000	460	3,460
	1,600	3,920	0	3,920
5	1,900	720	1,900	2,620
	1,900	1,500	1,510	3,010
	1,900	2,500	1,010	3,510
	1,900	4,520	0	4,520
6**	2,200	720	2,200	2,920
	2,200	1,500	1,810	3,310
	2,200	3,000	1,060	4,060
	2,200	5,120	0	5,120

* It is expected that states paying more than the federal guarantee in their public assistance programs will supplement federal guarantee up to its present level.

** Add $300 to guarantee for each additional child.

$1600 payment. A 50 percent tax rate would be applied to earnings above this amount, so that as earnings increased, the assistance payment would be decreased, but not until the income level of $3920 for a family of four was reached would the family be ineligible for assistance. States which now pay more than $1600 for a family of four would be expected and helped by the federal government to continue paying up to their present standard, so that no family would be worse off than it is under the present AFDC program. Poor families without dependent children are not covered by this program and would have to continue to look to the public assistance programs for the blind, aged, and disabled.

The president has proposed that a food stamp bonus be added to the minimum Family Assistance payment, bringing the minimum guarantee for a family of four up to about $2400, about $800 of which would be food stamps. At the present time there appear to be myriad problems involved in integrating the two programs. They are being administered by two different agencies. Legislation in each of the programs is initiated by different congressional committees. The food stamp program is not funded at levels that can cover the potential Family Assistance target population. These problems as well as other considerations discussed in this book indicate that it would be preferable to raise the cash guarantee of the Family Assistance Plan to $2400 for a family of four and to eliminate the food stamp program for these families. The food stamp program could be maintained for those not eligible for Family Assistance, with the idea that eventually these households too would be eligible for a cash assistance program.

The President's Commission on Income Maintenance Programs, appointed by President Johnson and continued by President Nixon, who received its report in November 1969, suggested that a cash assistance program for needy households be initiated at the $2400 level (for a family of four). The commission pointed out many of the problems involved in administering in-kind programs which, in effect, attempt to make expenditure decisions for poor households. It suggested the food programs be eliminated and emphasized the efficiency and equity of cash payments.

82

If we reduce the problem of poverty to its essential nature, we find it is simply the relative lack of choice. In this respect we are all poor to some degree, for we all want more than we can afford. On the other hand, most of us have the opportunity to choose a life style which we recognize to be far above the minimum needed to preserve our physical and mental health. The poor lack the opportunity to choose even this minimum environment.

America is at the crossroads. With our next step we can perpetuate the caste system that has separated the poor from the rest of society and denied them the opportunities that participation in that society has brought to the rest of us, or we can establish a system which gives a sizable group of our citizens the most precious right our society has to offer—the freedom to choose the elements of one's own life style.

The price of a fair and adequate system of income security for the poor is not low, but the cost of not having one is inordinately high, for only when we can assure that all our citizens have the opportunity for self-respect can we preserve our own self-respect.

BIBLIOTHÈQUE CHAMPLAIN

3 9365 00201525 5